ALLAH, THE Q

ALLAH, THE QURAN, VENUS AND YOU

Published by Zoser Research Society

www.zoserresearchsociety.com

Copyright 2019 by Kedar Griffo

ISBN

Front and back cover by Tehuti Re

Painted Pictures by Emhotep Gerald Richards at www.nuwbia.com; Harmonia Rosales www.harmoniarosales.com

All rights reserved. No part of this book may be reproduced, stored in retrieval system or transmitted in any form, by any means, including mechanical, electronic, photocopying, recording, or otherwise without prior written permission of the publisher.

Printed in the United States of America.

Books authored

African Origin Found in Religion and Freemasonry Part 1

African Origin Found in Religion and Freemasonry Part 2

Do Freemasons Worship Lucifer?

God, The Bible, The Planets, and Your Body

Out of Egypt, The Story of Blacks In The Bible

Religion, Politics and Freemasonry, A Violent Attack Against Ancient Africa

The Debate: Zoser Research Society Vs. Phylaxis Research Society

ABOUT THE AUTHOR

Dr. Kedar Griffo is the founder of Zoser Research Society and has authored eight books on subjects ranging from ancient cosmologies, politics, occult sciences and finances. He received his honorary Doctor of Divinity in Comparative Religious Studies from Holy Tabernacle Ministries. He is a sought-after public speaker who has appeared on the small screen co-hosting a television program as well as co-hosting a radio broadcast. He is a multi-decorated desert storm veteran with over 30 years of public service.

Author's Acknowledgements

While you can never thank everyone, who has a hand in realizing this book to completion, there are a few individuals whose works have made this book possible. From book cover designers and models to the dedicated editors and lastly the authors of other books that I was able to read and from whom I continue to learn. My travel agent who helped me secure my experience and expedition to the Holy Land, Tama-Re aka Egypt for research purposes.

A special thank you goes to black bookstores without you, we would have no platform. Currently those black bookstores that carry this book and my other publications are: Medu Bookstore (Nia Damali), Nubian Bookstore (Marcus Williams), Black Dot Bookstore and Cultural Center (Adigun Kazemde Ajamu), Shrine of the Black Madonna Atlanta Location, Luxor Couture Bookstore (Kerf) and Alkebu-lan bookstore (Yusef Harris)

Eternal gratitude goes to my family and friends who have allowed me to forsake communion in an effort to complete this work. I apologize a thousand times and will make it up to you.

Chef Otis Wagner aka Hutip Sen Sabaq (PBUH) you were the true definition of a peacemaker may the ancestors guide your journey home. Thank you for blessing our encounters

Lastly and surely not least we want to thank you the reader for purchasing, recommending, sharing and discussing the contents of this book with friends, family, associates and enemies.

ALLAH, THE QURAN, VENUS AND YOU

Table of Contents

Islam in America – page 17

Venus Islam -- page 36

Venus – Mars -- page 44

Islam and Astrology -- page 73

Essential Oils -- page 91

Lord of Sirius – 72

Red Black and White -- 97

DEDICATION

This book is dedicated to my maternal matriarch, Francis Izora Lloyd nee Wilder. The name Izora means dawn, aurora, sunrise in the Slavic language. Momma Zola, as she was with great affection known by her grandchildren and others in her neighborhood, bore five children, Lois, Odis Jr, Dorothy, Joanne and Shirley who has since joined the ancestral realm. Momma Zola was the daughter of Emma and Willie Wilder and like most Africans in America had native American ancestry. She descended from the Mende tribe of Mandelay known know as Sierra Leone, Africa. Her family migrated from North Carolina to Arkansas during the time of the Trail of Tears. Migration from the original Cherokee Nation began in the early 1800's. Some Cherokees left the east coast because of white encroachment and moved west on their own and settled in other areas of the country. A group of Cherokees known as the Old Settlers moved in 1817 to lands given to them in Arkansas where they established a government and a peaceful way of life. Later, however, some were forced to migrate to Oklahoma and further west. One of her earliest ancestors was a man named Frank Harris from North Carolina, who was from the Gullah misnomer Geechee people of the low country in South Carolina. In the early 1800's President Thomas Jefferson spoke to a Cherokee delegation about "vacant lands" in 1809 when he invited those wishing to move to go to the country on the waters of the Arkansas and White Rivers which is near Ethel Arkansas her place of birth.

Momma Zola was skilled in ancient ancestral arts and practices. She could utter a phrase and stop nose bleeds. She also instructed her children on how to stop or slow hemorrhaging. She taught her children about the stars and their relationship to their bodies. Never allowing them to have dental procedures when the moon was in astrological sign of Capricorn. Therefore, it is with this knowledge, which has been passed down to me through my mother Joanne, that I offer you some of this same ancestral wisdom from my maternal grandmother about the stars, our bodies and how they are interrelated and connected.

INTRODUCTION

This scroll intends to elaborate on the presence of the solar system, zodiac and the human body as it relates to the Religion of Islam, its God called in Arabic, Allah and its holy book, the Quran. Allah is the Arabic name for the Supreme Being, 1702, Alha, from Arabic Allah, contraction of al-Ilah, literally "the God," from al "the" + Ilah "God," which is cognate with Aramaic elah, Hebrew eloah (see Elohim). Etyomology Online 3/8/2019. https://www.etymonline.com/word/Allah#etymonline_v_8165 Eloah is the feminine word meaning Goddess or female God. A shorten version of Elohim is El. This word Allah sometimes written as Allat takes on both feminine and masculine as qualities. Therefore, this offering will alternate between the feminine and masculine aspects of this word.

     The religion of Islam is more closely related to the planet Venus than Mars, however there are references to Mars found within the pages of the Quran which will be discussed later. For now, the planet Venus plays a prominent role in the formation of the religion of Islam called Din Allah in Arabic. According to the book Pathways to Astronomy, "Venus is named for the Roman goddess of love. From our perspective on Earth, Venus's smaller orbit (at about 0.72 AU) never carries it father than 48 degrees from the Sun. For a period of about 9 to 10 months, we see it as a very bright "evening star" that sets after the Sun by as much as three hours. Then, after Venus moves along its orbit and passes between the Earth and the Sun, it reappears as a "morning star" for another 9 to 10 months. After it passes behind the Sun, Venus again appears as an evening star." Schneider, Stephen (2009). Pathways to Astrology: New York, NY McGraw-Hill Companies Publishing. p. 304. ISBN 978-0-07-340445-5

ALLAH, THE QURAN, VENUS AND YOU

      Venus is the second planet from the Sun and orbits the sun every 224.7 days. Venus has a very slow rotation and takes the longest amount of time of any planet in the solar system to rotate on its axis at 243 days. An interesting aspect of the planet Venus is it spins clockwise which means the sun would rise in the west and set in the east. This is known as retrograde rotation. Venus goes retrograde roughly once a year. Retrograde means it appears to orbit backwards. This retrograde lasts about six weeks or 40 days. Mars is the fourth planet from the Sun and orbits the sun every 687 days and takes 40 minutes more than an earth day to rotate on its axis. It is the second smallest planet in the solar system after Mercury if Pluto is no longer considered a planet. Author Stephen E. Schneider states "Mars is named for the Roman god of war, presumably because of its "blood red" color". Schneider, Stephen (2009). Pathways to Astrology: New York, NY McGraw-Hill Companies Publishing. p. 311. ISBN 978-0-07-340445-5

      Islamic history relays the Quran which is defined in the Arabic language to mean "reading" was sent down to the Prophet Muhammad over a period of 23 years. The Quran has 114 books. Muhammad met the Arch Angel Gabriel (Jibraiyl in the Arabic language) in a cave to receive revelations of the Quran in the year 610 A.D. Muhammad was born January 1, 570 A.D. and was the son of Amiynah and Abdullat. Muhammad's father, Abdullat, died almost six months before he was born. Muhammad was a member of the Quraysh tribe whose symbol was the fish. He was married multiple times; however, his first marriage was to a rich woman named Khadijah which lasted about 25 years. Khadijah was the cousin of Waraqa, a catholic priest, who wanted to control trade in Mecca by giving Arabs a revised form of Christianity. Waraqa was taught and influenced by St. Augustine. Muhammad had thirteen wives in total, his last wife being Aisha. According to some reports he had four daughters with Khadijah: Ruqayyah bint Muhammad, Umm Kulthum bint Muhammad, Zainab bint Muhammad, and Fatimah Zahra, as well as, two sons Abd-Allah ibn Muhammad and Qasim ibn Muhammad, who both died in childhood. All but one of his daughters, Fatimah, died before him. Another version of Islam says that Muhammad only had one daughter, Fatimah Zahra. Another of his wives, Maria Al Qibtiyya, had a son named Ibrahin ibn Muhammad who died in infancy.

The Prophet Muhammad (PBUH)

ALLAH, THE QURAN, VENUS AND YOU

Muhammad's daughter by Khadijah, Fatimah, also called Zahra and at times combined to be called Fatimah Zahra which some translate as Lady of Light, was married to Muhammad's nephew Ali. Fatimah Zahra sometimes called Zahra which translates as the shining one. This word, Zahra, has the same etymological roots as my grandmothers name Izora and both have meanings dealing with shining and being bright. Interestingly, the planet Venus has the same root letters of ZHR as Zahra. The Arabic word Zuhra which means Venus is from the root (z-h-r); compare (zahara, "to shine"). The definition of the word etymologically is seen as borrowed from Arabic (az-zuhara). Proper noun زهرة (zuhra) Venus the planet) References András J. E. Bodrogligeti, *A Grammar of Chagatay* (2001) (Zuhra) زَهْرَة Zahra means flower in the Arabic language. A similar spelling with the same meaning

is the word *Azhar*, which is an Arabic name for boys that means "brilliant", "radiant", "luminous."

Zohra is an indirect Quranic name for girls that means radiant white color. *Zohra* is also the Arabic word for the planet Venus. It is derived from the Z-H-R root which is used once in the Quran in the phrase *zahratul hayat*: "and never turn thine, eyes [with longing] towards whatever splendor of this world's life We may have allowed so many others to enjoy in order that We might test them thereby: for the sustenance which thy Lord provides [for thee] is better and more enduring," (Quran 20:131).

وَلَا تَمُدَّنَّ عَيْنَيْكَ إِلَى مَا مَتَّعْنَا بِهِ أَزْوَاجًا مِّنْهُمْ زَهْرَةَ الْحَيَاةِ الدُّنْيَا لِنَفْتِنَهُمْ فِيهِ وَرِزْقُ رَبِّكَ خَيْرٌ وَأَبْقَىٰ

Although Islam has been in existence since at least 632 A.D. most westerners are just now becoming familiar with the last of the Abrahamic faiths because of the Western world's war of Terrorism. Islam is one of the fastest growing religions in the western world and has grown exponentially in Northern America. Islam boasts is it not a compulsory religion. Adherents of Islam are called Muslims and are obligated to abide by five tenets or pillars. The five pillars are:

- Shahadah - Belief in the Oneness of God and the prophethood of Muhammad
- Selah - Establishment of the daily prayers
- Zakah - Concern for and almsgiving to the needy
- Sawm - Self-purification through fasting
- Hajj - The pilgrimage to Mecca for those who are able

Five Pillar of Islam

These five pillars are not found or listed together in the Quran, the Islamic holy book. The first of these pillars is the Shahadah which consists of making a declaration bearing witness that "there is no God but Allah and Allah has no partners and is alone. Muslims say in Arabic, La Ilah Ila Allah." This is similar to the Hebraic phrase Shema Yisrael, Adonai Elohim Adonai ekhad which translates as "Hear, O' Israel: The Lord our God, the Lord is One," as found in the book of Deuteronomy 6:4-5. שְׁמַע, יִשְׂרָאֵל: יְהוָה אֱלֹהֵינוּ, יְהוָה אֶחָד.

The Quran has a similar saying and says in Surah 3:18

شَهِدَ اللَّهُ أَنَّهُ لَا إِلَٰهَ إِلَّا هُوَ وَالْمَلَائِكَةُ وَأُولُو الْعِلْمِ قَائِمًا بِالْقِسْطِ ۚ لَا إِلَٰهَ إِلَّا هُوَ الْعَزِيزُ الْحَكِيمُ

Allah witnesses that there is no deity except Him, and [so do] the angels and those of knowledge - [that He is] maintaining [creation] in justice. There is no deity except Him, the Exalted in Might, the Wise.

Prayer or salat is next of the five pillars of Islam. We appointed for Abraham the location of the House, "Do not associate anything with Me and purify My House for the visitors and those who stand, bow and prostrate." 22:26

وَإِذْ بَوَّأْنَا لِإِبْرَاهِيمَ مَكَانَ الْبَيْتِ أَن لَّا تُشْرِكْ بِي شَيْئًا وَطَهِّرْ بَيْتِيَ لِلطَّائِفِينَ وَالْقَائِمِينَ وَالرُّكَّعِ السُّجُودِ -

And [mention, O Muhammad], when We designated for Abraham the site of the House, [saying], "Do not associate anything with Me and purify My House for those who perform Tawaf and those who stand [in prayer] and those who bow and prostrate.

The third of the pillars is Zakat or charity. We made them leaders who guide by Our command and We inspired them to work good deeds, to observe the Salat and to give the Zakat, they were worshippers of Us. 21:73

وَجَعَلْنَاهُمْ أَئِمَّةً يَهْدُونَ بِأَمْرِنَا وَأَوْحَيْنَا إِلَيْهِمْ فِعْلَ الْخَيْرَاتِ وَإِقَامَ الصَّلَاةِ وَإِيتَاءَ الزَّكَاةِ وَكَانُوا لَنَا عَابِدِينَ –

The "Fourth pillar of Islam" is the Fasting of the month of Ramadan. As with all other practices, all the details of Fasting are given in the Quran. " It has been made permissible for you the night preceding fasting to go to your wives [for sexual relations]. They are clothing for you and you are clothing for them. Allah knows that you used to deceive yourselves, so He accepted your repentance and forgave you. So now, have relations with them and seek that which Allah has decreed for you. You may eat and drink until the white thread becomes distinguishable to you from the dark thread at dawn. Then you shall maintain the fast until the night. 2:187

أُحِلَّ لَكُمْ لَيْلَةَ الصِّيَامِ الرَّفَثُ إِلَىٰ نِسَائِكُمْ ۚ هُنَّ لِبَاسٌ لَّكُمْ وَأَنتُمْ لِبَاسٌ لَّهُنَّ ۗ عَلِمَ اللَّهُ أَنَّكُمْ كُنتُمْ تَخْتَانُونَ أَنفُسَكُمْ فَتَابَ عَلَيْكُمْ وَعَفَا عَنكُمْ ۖ فَالْآنَ بَاشِرُوهُنَّ وَابْتَغُوا مَا كَتَبَ اللَّهُ لَكُمْ ۚ وَكُلُوا وَاشْرَبُوا حَتَّىٰ يَتَبَيَّنَ لَكُمُ الْخَيْطُ الْأَبْيَضُ مِنَ الْخَيْطِ الْأَسْوَدِ مِنَ الْفَجْرِ ۖ ثُمَّ أَتِمُّوا الصِّيَامَ إِلَى اللَّيْلِ ۚ وَلَا تُبَاشِرُوهُنَّ وَأَنتُمْ عَاكِفُونَ فِي الْمَسَاجِدِ ۗ تِلْكَ حُدُودُ اللَّهِ فَلَا تَقْرَبُوهَا ۗ كَذَٰلِكَ يُبَيِّنُ اللَّهُ آيَاتِهِ لِلنَّاسِ لَعَلَّهُمْ يَتَّقُونَ

The last and most difficult of the pillars for Muslims that do not live in the Arabian Peninsula is Hajj. Surah Baqarah says The Hajj is during the known months. 2:197

الْحَجُّ أَشْهُرٌ مَّعْلُومَاتٌ ۚ فَمَن فَرَضَ فِيهِنَّ الْحَجَّ فَلَا رَفَثَ وَلَا فُسُوقَ وَلَا جِدَالَ فِي الْحَجِّ ۗ وَمَا تَفْعَلُوا مِنْ خَيْرٍ يَعْلَمْهُ اللَّهُ ۗ وَتَزَوَّدُوا فَإِنَّ خَيْرَ الزَّادِ التَّقْوَىٰ ۚ وَاتَّقُونِ يَا أُولِي الْأَلْبَابِ

Hajj is [during] well-known months, so whoever has made Hajj obligatory upon himself therein [by entering the state of ihram], there is [to be for him] no sexual relations and no disobedience and no disputing during Hajj. And whatever good you do - Allah knows it. And take provisions, but indeed, the best provision is fear of Allah. And fear Me, O you of understanding.

    According to the book the Degree of Muhammadism, "There was a group of people call the Sabeans who inhabited Syria and existed thousands of years before Muhammad. The Sabeans were Christians who worshipped Stars and their religion was called the religion of Sabi and they had a Quiblah (direction of prayer) facing south of Syria. Sabi means one who has departed from one religion to another. The Arabs used to refer to Muhammad as a Sabi, because he departed from the so called paganistic religion of the Quraysh to Al Islam. t/he word Sabean is used in the Quran three times: Surahs 2:50, 5;73 and 22.17. Some people refer to the Sabeans as the Mandaeans, who followed Persian, Gnostic, Jewish and

Christian doctrines, and heavily influenced St. Augustine who influenced Islam. These Mandaeans practiced baptism as well as the other groups of Sabians or Harran (Syria) worshipped the stars and admitted the existence of astral spirits. Among the spirits are to be found administrators of the seven planets that are like temples according to Islamic scholar Al Sharastani. One group of Sabians worshipped the stars called temple directly: and the other group worshipped handmade idols representing the stars in temples made by man." It goes on to say the Sabians had influenced the rites and ceremonies of the so-called pagan Meccans. For instance, the keeping of 360 idols in the Ka'aba and ceremony of circling the Ka'aba seven times is symbolic of the motion of the seven planets, - which all came from the Sabians. Rooakhptah Amunnubi, The Degree of Muhummadism, Tama-Re Publishing, 2001, p. 40.

Islam in America

Islam has been in America before Europeans invaded America. Historian Ivan Van Sertima stated in his books "They Came Before Columbus" and "African Presence in Early America" there were African Muslim settlements in the Americas, before the expedition of Columbus. However, for the sake of brevity we will briefly discuss the Muslims leaders in America from the early 20th century who were responsible for teaching Islam in America. One of the first of these Islamic teachers was an Egyptian named Duse Muhammad Ali. He was born November 21, 1866 and transitioned on June 25, 1945. He mentored the Most Honorable Marcus Mosiah Garvey of the United Negro Improvement Association (UNIA). The young Marcus Garvey, then studying in London from Jamaica, frequently visited Ali's Fleet Street office and was mentored by him. David Dabydeen, John Gilmore, Cecily Jones (eds), *The Oxford Companion to Black British History*, Oxford University Press, 2007, p. 25.

Duse Ali

Duse Ali was also said to have influenced Noble Drew Ali of the Moorish Science Temple of America. Noble Drew Ali is another of Islamic leaders in America in the early 20th century. He was born on a Cherokee reservation in North Carolina in January 8, 1886 and departed his earthly body on July 20, 1929. He founded the Canaanite Temple in Newark, NJ in the year 1913. Later, he moved to Chicago and incorporated the Moorish Science Temple No. 9 in 1925. Noble Drew Ali taught Master Fard Muhammad seen in the image below in the top left-hand corner of the photo directly under the lamp post. Master Fard Muhammad left the MSTA and taught The Most Honorable Elijah Muhammad in Detroit.

Moorish Science Temple of America (MSTA)

ALLAH, THE QURAN, VENUS AND YOU

According to the teachings of the Nation of Islam, Wallace D. Fard came to America from Mecca in 1930. He used the name of Wallace D. Ford, often signing in W.D. Fard. In the third year (1933) he signed his name W.F. Muhammad which stands for Wallace Fard Muhammad. "Muhammad, Elijah, The University of Islam, Chicago, Illinois, 1957, The Supreme Wisdom, Page 11" Master Fard Muhammad appeared to the Honorable Elijah Muhammad in Detroit, Michigan in 1931. He said he was a reincarnation of Noble Drew Ali. For the next three years, Elijah is a student of Fard Muhammad. Once Fard disappears, Elijah directs the Nation of Islam until his death in 1975. Out of all the leaders of Islam in America, The Honorable Elijah Muhammad is probably the most known. As the founder of the Nation of Islam he opened businesses, schools and temples all over America.

The Honorable Elijah Muhammad was responsible for greats like Muhammad Ali, Malcolm X, the Honorable Louis Farrakhan and the late Dr. Khalid Abdul Muhammad, who led the new Black Panther Party until his death in 2001 in Atlanta, Georgia. In the photo seated with glasses is The Honorable Elijah Muhammad, standing to his right is Malcolm X, and to the left standing is a young minister Louis Farrakhan, current leader of the Nation of Islam.

The Honorable Elijah Muhammad

Elijah's influence has been felt deep within the black community not only in America but internationally. Unbeknownst to many black people in America, the Honorable Elijah Muhammad met with the great Dr. Martin Luther King, Jr and discussed the plight of black people in America during the civil rights movement.

ALLAH, THE QURAN, VENUS AND YOU

Dr. Martin Luther King, Jr

The current leader of the Nation of Islam is the Honorable Louis Farrakhan who has been leader of the NOI since the late 1970s after he split from Elijah Muhammad's son, Warith Deen Muhammad. Farrakhan has been linked with former President of the United States, Barak Hussein Obama who has been accused of being a Muslim because his father was a Muslim from Kenya.

44th President, Barack Hussein Obama

One of the first Islamic teachers in America in the 20th century was Shaikh Daoud Ahmad Faisal who was born in Fez, Morocco in 1891 and eventually moved with his family to Antigua, West Indies in 1901 then finally to America in March 15, 1907. He was leader of a mosque he founded on State Street in Brooklyn, NY. He was a contemporary of Noble Drew Ali of the Moorish Science Temple of America (MSTA) and Fard Muhammad. Sheikh Daoud was also initiated into a Sufi Order called the *Alawiyya*, This Sufi order was created by Shaikh Ahmad Al Alawi who was from Algeria. Shaikh Al Alawi was a student of Darqawi Shaykh Muhammad al-Buzidi of Morrocco in the late 1894.

Shaikh Daoud influenced Malcolm X after his split from the Nation of Islam.   Another of Shaikh Daoud's students was called As Sayyid Al Imam Isa Al Haadi Al Mahdi or Imaam Isa for short. According to the book Shaikh Daoud Vs. Fard "He received a charter from Shaikh Daoud to teach Islam in America under the title Ansaar Allah Community on November 11, 1972." York, Malachi, Imaam Isa wrote hundreds of books and even translated the Quran to help teach Americans Muslims the arabic language. His community spoke arabic and dressed in traditional sudanese attire which linked them to the Ansaars of the Sudan. Following the lead of the Most Honorable Elijah Muhammad, Imaam Isa established businesses temples and bookstores all over the United States, Caribbean and the U.K. Initially the Ansaar Community was based in Brooklyn, like Shaikh Daouds mission however the headquarters eventually moved to upstate New York. Like his mentor Shaikh Daoud, Imaam Isa followed a sufi version of Islam and taught his followers the mystic and estoreric versions of Islam.

ALLAH, THE QURAN, VENUS AND YOU

Sheikh Daoud/Imaam Isa

ALLAH, THE QURAN, VENUS AND YOU

Imaam Isa/Sheik Daoud

Now that I have acquainted you with some of the first teachers of Islam in America, lets dissect the religion of Islam. This examination will not be viewed from the false narrative as told from Islamophobes in the media but by from an esoteric view and those that have practiced the religion of Islam.

In our book, God, the Bible, the Planets and Your Body we discussed the zodiac's influence on the bible and your body. The same authors that wrote the bible also wrote the Quran, thus the same writing style and influence will be seen in the Quran. The Quran mentions the ancient practice of meditation. Surah Al Nisa (woman) [4.82] Do they not then meditate on the Quran? And if it were from any other than Allah, they would have found in it many a discrepancy.

أَفَلَا يَتَدَبَّرُونَ الْقُرْآنَ ۚ وَلَوْ كَانَ مِنْ عِندِ غَيْرِ اللَّهِ لَوَجَدُوا فِيهِ اخْتِلَافًا كَثِيرًا

And in Surah [4.108] They hide themselves from men and do not hide themselves from Allah, and He is with them when they meditate by night words which please Him not, and Allah encompasses what they do.

يَسْتَخْفُونَ مِنَ النَّاسِ وَلَا يَسْتَخْفُونَ مِنَ اللَّهِ وَهُوَ مَعَهُمْ إِذْ يُبَيِّتُونَ مَا لَا يَرْضَىٰ مِنَ الْقَوْلِ ۚ وَكَانَ اللَّهُ بِمَا يَعْمَلُونَ مُحِيطًا

Like the God of the Bible; Allah, the God of the Quran, also speaks in parables

The Thunder [13.17] He sends down water from the cloud, then watercourses flow (with water) according to their measure, and the torrent bears along the swelling foam, and from what they melt in the fire for the sake of making ornaments or apparatus arises a scum like it; thus does Allah compare truth and falsehood; then as for the scum, it passes away as a worthless thing; and as for that which profits the people, it tarries in the earth; thus does Allah set forth **parables**.

أَنزَلَ مِنَ السَّمَاءِ مَاءً فَسَالَتْ أَوْدِيَةٌ بِقَدَرِهَا فَاحْتَمَلَ السَّيْلُ زَبَدًا رَّابِيًا ۚ وَمِمَّا يُوقِدُونَ عَلَيْهِ فِي النَّارِ ابْتِغَاءَ حِلْيَةٍ أَوْ مَتَاعٍ زَبَدٌ مِّثْلُهُ ۚ كَذَٰلِكَ يَضْرِبُ اللَّهُ الْحَقَّ وَالْبَاطِلَ ۚ فَأَمَّا الزَّبَدُ فَيَذْهَبُ جُفَاءً ۖ وَأَمَّا مَا يَنفَعُ النَّاسَ فَيَمْكُثُ فِي الْأَرْضِ ۚ كَذَٰلِكَ يَضْرِبُ اللَّهُ الْأَمْثَالَ

Abraham [14.25] Yielding its fruit in every season by the permission of its Lord? And Allah sets forth parables for men that they may be mindful.

تُؤْتِي أُكُلَهَا كُلَّ حِينٍ بِإِذْنِ رَبِّهَا ۗ وَيَضْرِبُ اللَّهُ الْأَمْثَالَ لِلنَّاسِ لَعَلَّهُمْ يَتَذَكَّرُونَ

The Light [24.35] Allah is the light of the heavens and the earth; a likeness of His light is as a niche in which is a lamp, the lamp is in a glass, (and) the glass is as it were a brightly shining star, lit from a blessed olive-tree, neither eastern nor western, the oil whereof almost gives light though fire touch it not-- light upon light-- Allah guides to His light whom He pleases, and Allah sets forth parables for men, and Allah is Cognizant of all things.

اللَّهُ نُورُ السَّمَاوَاتِ وَالْأَرْضِ ۚ مَثَلُ نُورِهِ كَمِشْكَاةٍ فِيهَا مِصْبَاحٌ ۖ الْمِصْبَاحُ فِي زُجَاجَةٍ ۖ الزُّجَاجَةُ كَأَنَّهَا كَوْكَبٌ دُرِّيٌّ يُوقَدُ مِن شَجَرَةٍ مُّبَارَكَةٍ زَيْتُونَةٍ لَّا شَرْقِيَّةٍ وَلَا غَرْبِيَّةٍ يَكَادُ زَيْتُهَا يُضِيءُ وَلَوْ لَمْ تَمْسَسْهُ نَارٌ ۚ نُّورٌ عَلَىٰ نُورٍ ۗ يَهْدِي اللَّهُ لِنُورِهِ مَن يَشَاءُ ۚ وَيَضْرِبُ اللَّهُ الْأَمْثَالَ لِلنَّاسِ ۗ وَاللَّهُ بِكُلِّ شَيْءٍ عَلِيمٌ

The Banishment [59.21] Had We sent down this Quran on a mountain, you would certainly have seen it falling down, splitting asunder because of the fear of Allah, and We set forth these parables to men that they may reflect.

لَوْ أَنزَلْنَا هَٰذَا الْقُرْآنَ عَلَىٰ جَبَلٍ لَّرَأَيْتَهُ خَاشِعًا مُّتَصَدِّعًا مِّنْ خَشْيَةِ اللَّهِ ۚ وَتِلْكَ الْأَمْثَالُ نَضْرِبُهَا لِلنَّاسِ لَعَلَّهُمْ يَتَفَكَّرُونَ

This informs the reader of the Quran that events cannot be taken literally as a parable means a usually short fictitious story that illustrates a moral attitude or a religious principle according to Merriam=Webster's online dictionary. https://www.merriam-webster.com/dictionary/parable taken 9/19/18.

Therefore, when one reads the Quran this view must be employed as it is with the Holy Bible. Let us began with an examination of the pillars of Islam, the first one called the Shahadah and sometimes called the Kalimah meaning word or declaration. When a Muslim takes their shahadah they say in Arabic La Ilaha Ila Allah which translates as There is no God but Allah. When you look at this saying in Arabic, you immediately notice it is four words which represent the four cardinal points the same as the four corners of the Kaaba. Second is the number of syllables in the kalimah is seven, representative of the seven visible planets, seven chakras and the number of circumambulations around the Kaaba. Lastly the kalimah in Arabic has 12 letters, for the 12 tribes of Ishmael, 12 cranial nerves and 12 zodiac signs.

Allah Ila Ilaha La

Kalimah/Shahadah

When Muslims say the amended Kalimah that includes the name of Muhammad it is seven syllables added to the 12 letters in La Ilaha Ila Allah and it equals 19. La Ilaha Ila Allah Muhammad rasulullah (There is not God but Allah and Muhammad is the messenger of Allah). Coincidently the Quran speaks of the number 19. [74.30] Over it are nineteen. عَلَيْهَا تِسْعَةَ عَشَرَ

Symbolic of the 12 zodiacs which are ruled by the seven visible planets. Added to the four words from the kalimah equals 23 (19+4) which equates to the amount of years the Quran was revealed to the prophet Muhammad. There are 114 surahs in the Quran which is a multiple of 19 (19 x 6); additional the number six is associated with Venus as the sixth day of the week called Jummah.

The second of these pillars is Salat which means prayer. There are five mandatory prayers throughout the day. The five obligatory prayers are Fajr – the dawn prayer, Dhuhr – noon prayer, Asr – afternoon prayer, Maghrib – sunset prayer and Isha'a the night prayer. Muslims pray towards the Qiblah or direction of prayer. Most think Muslims pray to the east which is partially true, However Muslims in nations east of Mecca would pray to the west. The Solstice points are used in determining the Qibla for orientation toward Mecca, in May 28/Nov. 28 (morning) versus in July 15/Jan. 13 (night). The Quran mentions seven prayer times. (Fajr – 30:17, Dhur – 30:18, Asr – 2:238, Maghrib – 30:17, Ishaa'a – 24-58, Ishraaq 38:18 and Tahajjud (17:78)

The times of prayers are based on the movement of the Sun in the sky. The morning prayer begins in the first house of the zodiac. The noon prayer called dhuhr is when the sun passes in the 9th house in the zodiac calendar and below the 7th house for the maghrib or sundown prayer. These five prayers also relate to the five senses and as we see later assist with aligning the chakras in the body. The most devout of Muslims have a mark on their foreheads called a prostration mark. When Muslims are in the prayer position called Sujud their forehead is placed on the ground. Notice this is the exact place of the 6th chakra called the brow chakra. In the bible it is referred to as the jewel in the forehead. Isaiah 3:20 "Jewel on thy forehead."

הַפְּאֵרִים וְהַצְּעָדוֹת וְהַקִּשֻּׁרִים, וּבָתֵּי הַנֶּפֶשׁ וְהַלְּחָשִׁים.

ALLAH, THE QURAN, VENUS AND YOU

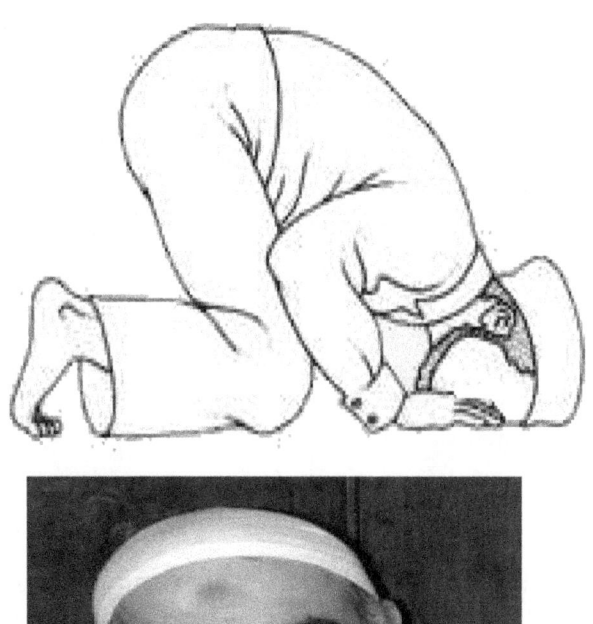

Prostration Mark

At pilgrimage the Hajjis dress in all white in a ceremonial dress called Ihrams. The Kaaba complex is shaped like the body of a female when it includes the Hatim. This design is the same as Solomon's temple, the temple of man in Luxor, Egypt or any of the many Vedic Hindu temple.

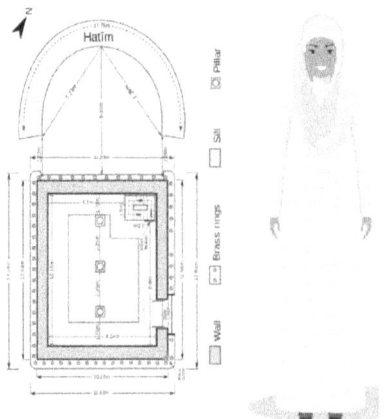 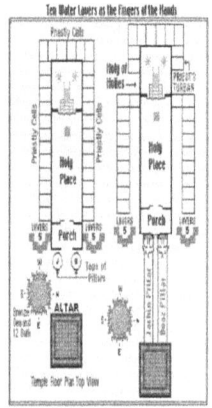

Hatim

When millions of pilgrims make Hajj, it resembles the reproductive act of millions of sperm trying to fertilize the ovum (egg). Just as Venus is the only planet in the solar system that rotates opposite the other eight planets, when Muslims make Hajj, they make an anti-clockwise circumambulation around the Kaaba resembling that of Hindus who march in the clockwise direction around their siva lingams. The siva lingam represents the fertility of the phallus and the yoni combined. The phallus resembles the minaret in Islam. The minaret and dome in Islam are the same as the siva lingam which is found in ancient Africa as the fertility deity Min.

ALLAH, THE QURAN, VENUS AND YOU

Siva Lingam

The most central focus of hajj is the Hajar Aswad or Black stone at the northeast corner of the Kaaba. Racist Muslims teach the black stone was originally white and became black because of the sin it absorbed. However, the black stone is a symbol of the Vedic god Shiva, so when millions of staunch and devout Muslims kiss the Black Stone, they kiss the sacred emblem of Shiva or the yoni. Unbeknownst to these patriarchs they are performing a ritual associated with sex and reproduction. The ihram which is white represents semen and the black stone shaped like the female reproductive organ leaves no doubt this is sexual and deals with the goddess of love, Venus. The Black Stone was broken into seven places and now is held together by a silver band, studded with silver nails. Silver is also associated with the planet Venus.

The Kaaba is patterned after the Tefillin found in the Hebrew/Jewish culture. The tefillin is a black cube  worn on the right forearm and the top of the head of orthodox Jews. On the forearm it is wrapped 13 times; 3 times around the bicep, 7 times around the forearm and 3 times around the fingers. The tefillin has three Hebrew letters Shin, Daleth and Alif which spell the Hebrew word Shaddai שַׁדַּי meaning "Almighty" as found in Genesis 28:3. This is also found in the Quran in Surah 53:5 The Lord of Mighty Power has taught him. Notice both scriptures Genesis 28:3 and Surah Al Najm (star) 53:5 add up to the number 13.

    Like the tefillin which has the words of God inside of the black box and the Torah commands the wearer to remember God, Exodus 13:9, "And it shall be for a sign for you upon your hand, and for a memorial between your eyes, that the law of the LORD may be in your mouth; for with a strong hand did the LORD bring you out of Egypt."

ט, וְהָיָה לְךָ לְאוֹת עַל-יָדְךָ, וּלְזִכָּרוֹן בֵּין עֵינֶיךָ, לְמַעַן תִּהְיֶה תּוֹרַת יְהוָה בְּפִיךָ: כִּי בְּיָד חֲזָקָה, הוֹצִאֲךָ יְהוָה מִמִּצְרָיִם.

    The Ka'aba has the words of God written on the kiswah, the black curtain, that covers the Ka'aba. A tribe called the Abbasids whose household color was black started this tradition, before that time it was covered in multiple colors including green, red and even white. Symbolically the Ka'aba or cube is one of the five platonic solids. The platonic solids were initially identified in Greek philosopher Plato book Timaeus, written around 350 BC. He described these five solids and correlated them to the five elements. The tetrahedron, containing four sides, represents fire. The cube, contains six sides, represents earth. The octahedron, has eight sides and represents air. The icosahedron has 20 sides for the element water. Finally, the dodecahedron, is made up of 12 sides representing the Kosmos. Esoterically the cube or tetrahedron represents the Ka'aba and earth. According to the Quran which states in Surah 2:127 and [mention] when Abraham was raising the foundations of the House and [with him] Ishmael, [saying], "Our Lord, accept [this] from us. Indeed, you are the Hearing, the Knowing."

وَإِذْ يَرْفَعُ إِبْرَاهِيمُ الْقَوَاعِدَ مِنَ الْبَيْتِ وَإِسْمَاعِيلُ رَبَّنَا تَقَبَّلْ مِنَّا ۖ إِنَّكَ أَنتَ السَّمِيعُ الْعَلِيمُ

Abraham represents the earth sign called Taurus which links Surah 2 called Baqarah meaning the cow in Arabic to the second zodiac sign Taurus. Surah Baqarah has 6,201(9) words and 25,500 (13) letters. Taurus is an earth sign so this association with the Ka'aba and Abraham should not be viewed lightly. The Ka'aba has six sides each totaling 360 degrees equaling 2,160 total degrees. This number is also symbolic of the total diameter of the moon, earths satellite, which is approximately 2,160 miles in diameter.

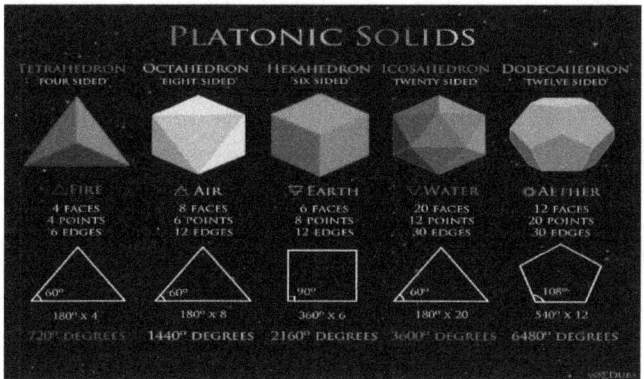

Platonic Solids

These platonic solids are also related to the five pillars of faith in Islam as well as the five senses. The Shahadah meaning to bear witness is related to the sense of seeing. Salat or prayer relates to hearing. Sawm or fasting deals with the sense of taste. Alms or giving deals is related to touch. Lastly, Hajj corresponds to smell.

VENUS/ISLAM

The religion of Islam was established over 1400 years ago in Mecca by the Arabian prophet Muhammad. It is the last of the Abrahamic faiths along with Judaism and Christianity. Like its predecessors, Islam has correspondences with the stars and our bodies. In our previous scroll, *God the Bible, the Planets and Your Body*, we showed you this correspondence and our goal is to show the same with Islam. Islam is based on a single deity named Allah which get its roots from the word Al Ilah and Eloah according to etymology online. Arabic name for the Supreme Being, 1702, Alha, from Arabic Allah, contraction of al-Ilah, literally "the God," from al "the" + Ilah "God," which is cognate with Aramaic elah, Hebrew eloah
https://www.etymonline.com/word/Allah#etymonline_v_8165

Allah like the God, Yahweh of the Holy Bible has been identified as a masculine deity, however the word Eloah as found in Hebrew is a feminine name. Eloah appears 57 times in the Old Testament; two-thirds of those mentions occur in the book of Job the oldest book in the bible. Another place in the bible where the word for God is feminine is El Shaddai. El means 'God'. The word shad means "woman's breast" [Strong's 7699], and Shaddai [7706] means "breasts", "breasted", or "many breasts."
http://www.eliyah.com/cgi-bin/strongs.cgi?file=hebrewlexicon&isindex=7699

Though El Shaddai is translated as "Almighty God", "God Almighty", or "the Almighty" in the English Bible, it literally means "God with breasts" or "[many] breasted [One] Shaddai or El Shaddai appears in the Old

Testament 48 times with 31 of those occurrences are found in the book of Job. El Shaddai is also found in the Quran in Surah 53.5 The Lord of Mighty Power has taught him. عَلَّمَهُ شَدِيدُ الْقُوَىٰ This shows the God of the Bible is the same as the God of the Quran. Yet the Hebrews did not know this God by this name according to the book of Exodus. Exodus 6:3: "To Abraham, Isaac and Jacob I appeared as El Shaddai, but I did not make my name Yahweh known to them; (And I appeared unto Abraham, unto Isaac, and unto Jacob, by the name of God Almighty, but by my name JEHOVAH was I not known to them".

וָאֵרָא, אֶל-אַבְרָהָם אֶל-יִצְחָק וְאֶל-יַעֲקֹב--בְּאֵל שַׁדָּי; וּשְׁמִי יְהוָה, לֹא נוֹדַעְתִּי לָהֶם.

The deity the Hebrews knew was the Goddess Eloah, or El Shaddai, a feminine deity. Antiquity has revealed the most ancient of deities were feminine, thus the god of the Quran is also feminine. Islamic legend says the ancient Arabian god was named Allat and she was the wife and or daughter of the god Allah. Famed historian Herodotus equated her with the deity Aphrodite who also shares attributes with Venus.

Aphrodite

In the Qur'an, she is mentioned along with al-'Uzzá and Manāt in Surah 53:19–23. In Arabic, Allah means 'God.' Similarly, Al-Lat means simply 'Goddess,' the supreme reality in female form. Muslims teach Muhammad destroyed all of the 360 idols found inside of the Kaaba (the black cube found in Mecca) inclusive of the goddess Allat and instituted worship of the one true god, Allah. However, the author's aim is to examine if that really occurred as a number of Islamic historical sites and concepts point to something different as it relates to male deities and Islam.

"Shrine of the sacred stone in Mecca, formerly dedicated to the pre-Islamic Triple Goddess Manat, Al-Lat (Allah), and Al-Uzza, the 'Old Woman' worshipped by Muhammed's tribesmen the Quraysh. The stone was also called Kubaba, Kuba or Kube, and has been linked with the name of Cybele (Kybela), the Great Mother of the Gods. The stone bore the emblem of the yoni, like the Black Stone worshipped by votaries of Artemis. Now it is regarded as the holy center of Islam, and its feminine symbolism has been lost, though priests of the Kaaba are still known as Sons of the Old Woman."
http://www.truthbeknown.com/islam.htm

The religion of Islam was the work of the Catholic church according to some. Author Tony Bushby says in his book The Crucifixion of Truth "Today he is called Mohammed (570-632), but his real name was Lothar Schmalfuss...his reference is found in a book called *Chronica Majora*, a summary of world history from biblical Creation to the year of the author's death. It was written by Matthew Paris (d.1259), a pious Christian monk, described by the church "as an historian who holds the first place among English chroniclers." From his quaint specimen of Abbey records, the erudite Monk explained how Mohammed started an "impious religion."

"It is well known that Mohammed was once a cardinal, and became heretic because he failed to be elected pope. Also (later in life) having drunk to excess, he fell by the roadside, and in this condition was killed by swine. And for that reason, his followers abhor pork even unto this day. Monk Matthew Paris called Mohammed 'cardinal'; a term that today signifies councillors of the pope, and the origin of that category of priesthood reveals another area of censored information in Christian development. The 16th Century church said that 'the office of cardinal (incardinatus) first came into being in the 6th Century...its true origin to this day remains unanswered for in none of the Councils (records) do we find authority for the distinguishing features of the office'. However, the position of cardinal was created by special decree at a French synod in January 560 and that information is recorded church history. 'The Synods which were held during the sixth century were confined to France and Spain"(The Crucifixion of the Truth, Tony Bushby, p. 166).

These Catholics were studiers and students of the occult mysteries including the science of astrology and the zodiac. The following image shows the Pope inclusive of cardinals being instructed on the mazzaroth, a Hebrew word for zodiac.

Pope learning Astrology

ISLAM AND ASTROLOGY

The Quran speaks against fortune telling which Muslims have concluded is Astrology. Surah Al-Maida 5:3 commands "Forbidden also is to use arrows seeking luck or decision; all that is disobedience of Allah and sin." In Arabic the word Buruj means constellations or zodiac signs like the Hebrew word Mazzaroth as found in the book of Job (Ayob in Arabic) 38.32. The Quran has a surah (chapter) named Buruj it is the 85th chapter and it is dedicated to the constellations or zodiac. Thus, the Quran could not be anti-astrology as most Muslims have been taught. The following verses are from the Quran and speaks about the zodiac.

- Surah 85:1 "I swear by the sky where there are buruj..."
  (Allah swears by the sky where there is zodiac signs.)

- Surah Hizr 15:16 "I have created buruj (Zodiac signs) on the sky and decorated them for viewers and I have also protected them from evils..."

- Surah Furkan 25:61 "How great he is, who has created buruj in the sky and placed the Sun and shining Moon over there..."

In Arabic the word for astrologer is munajjim, Astrology is Ilm an-Nujūm and the word for astronomy is Ilm al-hay'ah Arabic for astronomy. Certain Muslim sects refer to the prophet Enoch or Idris in Arabic as the founder of the science of the stars.

ALLAH, THE QURAN, VENUS AND YOU

This knowledge of the sun, stars and moon was also incorporated into certain surahs in the Quran. For example, there is a surah dedicated to the sun entitled As Shams which is Surah 91. Surah 54 or Al Qumra is dedicated to the moon. Thus, it is hard to not see that the holiest book in all of Islam is not an ode to the solar system, planets and zodiac. The Islamic alphabet has 28 letters, divided into sun and moon letters. 14 for the waxing moon or right hand and 14 for the waning moon or left hand which equates to one letter for each day of the 28-day lunar month.

Sun letters   ت ث د ذ ر ز س ش ص ض ط ظ ل ن
               t   *th*   *d*   *dh*   *r*   *z*   *s*   *sh*   *s*   *d*   *t*   *z*   *l*   *n*

Moon letters   ء ب ج ح خ ع غ ف ق ك م و ي ه
               '   *b*   *j*   *h*   *kh*   *'*   *gh*   *f*   *q*   *k*   *m*   *w*   *y*   *h*

SUN/MOON Letters

On occasions, you will see Muslims holding what looks like rosary beads, they are very similar in purpose and are called dhikr beads they are usually 33 in number. This relates to the 33 vertebrates in the spinal column just as the 28 letters in the alphabet related to the 14 phalanges on the hands and feet.

ALLAH, THE QURAN, VENUS AND YOU

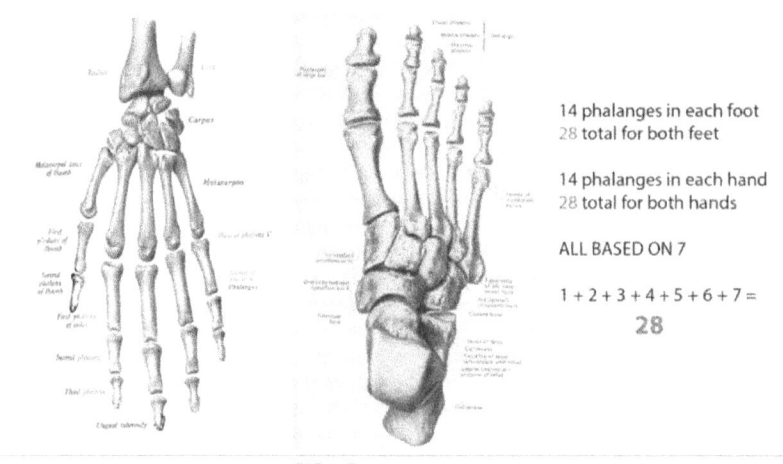

14 phalanges in each foot
28 total for both feet

14 phalanges in each hand
28 total for both hands

ALL BASED ON 7

1 + 2 + 3 + 4 + 5 + 6 + 7 =
28

Phalanges

There are 12 sons of Ishmael which parallel the 12 sons of Israel. Genesis 25:13 And these [are] the names of the sons of Ishmael, by their names, according to their generations: the firstborn of Ishmael, Nebajoth (meaning to be high or prominent, heights); and Kedar (meaning to be dark), and Adbeel (meaning chastened or *grieved by God*), and Mibsam (meaning sweet odor) , 14 And Mishma (meaning a hearing), and Dumah (meaning silence), and Massa (meaning burden), 15 Hadar (meaning honor), and Tema (meaning desert), Jetur (meaning enclosed), Naphish(meaning refreshment) and Kedemah (meaning original): 16 These [are] the sons of Ishmael

וְאֵלֶּה ,שְׁמוֹת בְּנֵי יִשְׁמָעֵאל ,בִּשְׁמֹתָם ,לְתוֹלְדֹתָם: בְּכֹר יִשְׁמָעֵאל נְבָיֹת ,וְקֵדָר וְאַדְבְּאֵל וּמִבְשָׂם

וּמִשְׁמָע וְדוּמָה ,וּמַשָּׂא

חֲדַד וְתֵימָא ,יְטוּר נָפִישׁ וָקֵדְמָה

ALLAH, THE QURAN, VENUS AND YOU

אֵלֶּה הֵם בְּנֵי יִשְׁמָעֵאל, וְאֵלֶּה שְׁמֹתָם, בְּחַצְרֵיהֶם, וּבְטִירֹתָם--
שְׁנֵים-עָשָׂר נְשִׂיאִם, לְאֻמֹּתָם

  Fortunately for Islam, there is a sect of Muslims who do not read the Quran literally and take it symbolically, they are known as Sufis like Shaikh Daoud and Imaam Isa. Online etymology dictionary defines Sufi "as a member of a Muslim mystical order. 1650s (earlier Sufian, 1580s) from Arabic Sufi, literally "man of wool" (i.e. man wearing woolen garments," as opposed to silk), from suf "wool." According to Klein, so-called from the habit of "putting on the holy garment" (labs-as-suf) to devote oneself to mysticism."
https://www.etymonline.com/word/Sufi#etymonline_v_223 19

Interesting the word Sufi is similar to the word Sophia meaning wisdom in Greek. In medical astrology known as Iastromathematics, Aries the ram (lamb) rules the head. Ram/Lamb wool wigs are worn by European judges as a sign of wisdom signifying those with lamb's wool also known as kinky/nappy hair are the true caretakers of wisdom. Sufi's seek various ways to enlightenment by employing the ancient practice of dhikr. The word dhikr is related to the Hebrew word for Adam called Zakar which means the rememberer. zakar: remember.
https://biblehub.com/hebrew/2142.htm

  Original Word: זָכַר
  Part of Speech: Verb
  Transliteration: zakar
  Phonetic Spelling: (zaw-kar')
  Short Definition: remember

  Thus, when Sufis dhikr, they are remembering Allah. Surah 29:45 states, "Recite that which has been revealed to you of the Book and keep up prayer; surely prayer keeps (one) away from indecency and evil, and certainly the remembrance of Allah is the greatest, and Allah knows what you do."

اتْلُ مَا أُوحِيَ إِلَيْكَ مِنَ الْكِتَابِ وَأَقِمِ الصَّلَاةَ ۖ إِنَّ الصَّلَاةَ تَنْهَىٰ عَنِ الْفَحْشَاءِ وَالْمُنْكَرِ ۗ وَلَذِكْرُ اللَّهِ أَكْبَرُ ۗ وَاللَّهُ يَعْلَمُ مَا تَصْنَعُونَ

They use the Dhikr method as a way to spiritual enlightenment and achieving union with Allah by chanting certain phrases. Chanting keeps the chakras tuned up and clear. Sufi's will chant *lā ilāha illa 'llāh*, "there is no god but God"; *Allāhu akbar*, "God is greatest"; *al-ḥamdu lī'llāh*, "praise be to God"; *astaghfiru 'llāh*, "I ask God's forgiveness"), and subhan Allah" are some chants that Muslim use when they dhikr or remember Allah. Chanting along with proper breathing and posture are all a part of the process when dhikring properly. Another ritual Sufis do is dance. Sufi dancers revolve around on their left foot with their head tilted as the earth's axis is tilted. The Sufi dancer is imitating the orbiting earth. The earth has a correspondence to the Pyramid of Khufu. Khufu Hellenized name is Sophis or Sofe a word very similar to the words Sufi and Sophia? Coincidence? Islam version of esotericism is Sufism and the Chakras are identified as *lataif-as-sitta* the six subtleties. These chakras are each assigned a frequency, a vibration that correspond to one of the notes of the octave. Arabic has seven vowels that correspond to these chakras. Thus, when one dhikrs they are aligning their chakras because they are using the very vowel sounds assigned to the seven chakras.

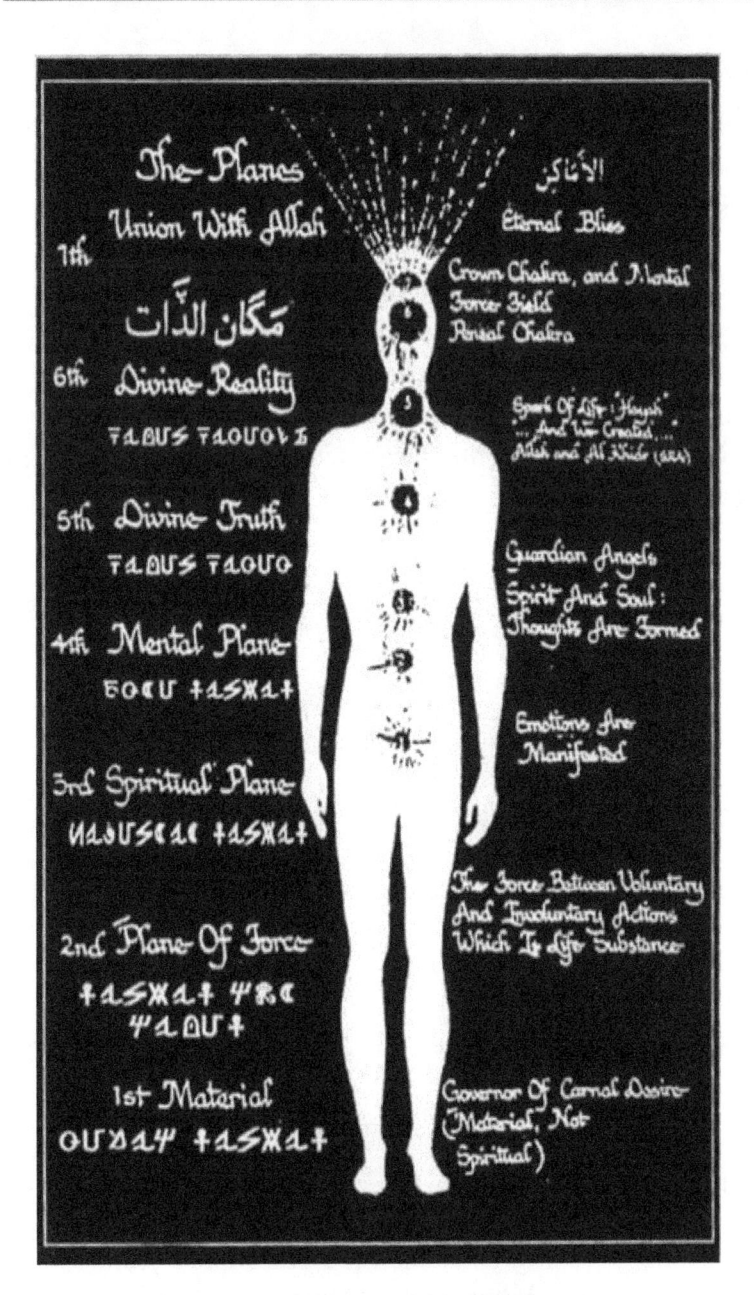

Seats of Lights/Chrakras

Vowel use is highly effective in balancing the chakras. Vowels have been used in many occult and mystery schools, including ancient Egyptians, Hebrew, Islamic, Tibetan, Japanese and Native American for chakra work. Unbeknownst to a lot of people learning about chakras, each vowel sound can be used to heal certain parts of the body and align the chakras if they happen to be unaligned. Manly P Hall states "From the writings of Aristotle and Hippocrates we know that as early as the 4th Century B.C.E. the Greek initiates attributed the seven vowels to the seven heavens and planets. [Manly P. Hall (1901-1990) in his *Secret Teachings of All Ages* discusses the correspondences: Manly P. Hall. *Secret Teachings of All Ages* (New York, NE:Tarcher/Penguin, 2003[1928]).

In the book Irenæus' *Against Heresies*, it states "The Greek initiates also recognized a fundamental relationship between the individual heavens or spheres of the seven planets, and the seven sacred vowels. The first heaven uttered the sound of the sacred vowel A (Alpha); the second heaven, the sacred vowel E (Epsilon); the third, H (Eta); the fourth, I (Iota); the fifth, O (Omicron); the sixth, Y (Upsilon); and the seventh heaven, the sacred vowel Ω (Omega). When these seven heavens sing together, they produce a perfect harmony which ascends as an everlasting praise to the throne of the Creator."
http://gnosis.org/library/advh1.htm

The seven Hebrew double letters (ב, ג, ד, כ, פ, ר, ת) map in their *alphabetic* order to the seven planets in their descending order of emanation (Saturn, Jupiter, Mars, Sun, Venus, Mercury, Moon). These seven vowels combined make the sound of the universe AUM or Om.

Vowel	(Saturn-Alpha)	(Moon – Alpha)
A , α	Saturn	Moon
E , ε	Jupiter	Mercury
H , η	Mars	Venus
I , ι	Sun	Sun
O , o	Venus	Mars
Y , υ	Mercury	Jupiter
Ω , ω	Moon	Saturn

Data from ESA (European Space Agency) and NASA's Solar and Heliospheric Observatory (SOHO) has captured the dynamic movement of the Sun's atmosphere for over 20 years. Today, we can hear the Sun's movement — all of its waves, loops and eruptions — with our own ears. This sound helps scientists study what can't be observed with the naked eye. "Waves are traveling and bouncing around inside the Sun, https://www.nasa.gov/feature/goddard/2018/sounds-of-the-sun

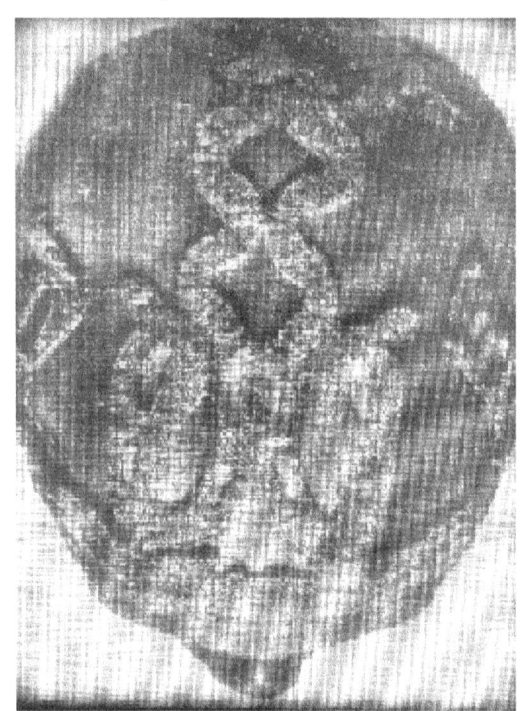

Aum, or Om is now introduced to you as Ohm is a frequency, vibration and sound. Once one aligns and activates the chakras it produces an electrical current that runs from the root to the crown chakra. Ancient Africans identified this thousands of years ago when they first decoded the human body. Thus, their iconography used snakes in the area of the forehead for the seat of light (See image of Tutankhamun) now referred to as the kundalini and djed pillars for the spinal column called sushumna in the Hindu language. The word sushumna means rich in pleasure. They identified the two snakes as the ida and pingala whose color was white and red respectively. The sushumna was black as it represented the spinal column. The great Mir (ancient Egyptian - Tama'rean word for pyramid) uses this color scheme in the great ascension temple called the great pyramid. The Mir was once covered in white limestone, the queens chamber was in white limestone and the kings chamber was in red granite. The Mir was not a burial chamber as Euro-Egyptologists exclaim to the world, it is a place to make spiritual ascension. The same way you should ascend the chakras from the root chakra to the crown chakra. This activation gives an electrical charge.

Everything we do is controlled and run by electrical signals running through our bodies. everything is made up of atoms which are comprised of protons, neutrons and electrons. Protons have a positive charge, neutrons have a neutral charge, and electrons have a negative charge. When these charges are not synced, our atoms give a negative or positive charge. The switch between the negative or positive charge allows electrons to flow from one atom to another. This flow of electrons, or a negative charge, is what we call electricity. Esoterically this was transferred from root chakra to the crown chakra via the kundalini and sushumna via energy tubes or channels called nadis. As this science was transferred throughout the African continent into Asia and the Americas, the colors (red, white, black) of these three became the basis of the current electrical wiring grid for most lighting, especially ceiling fans.

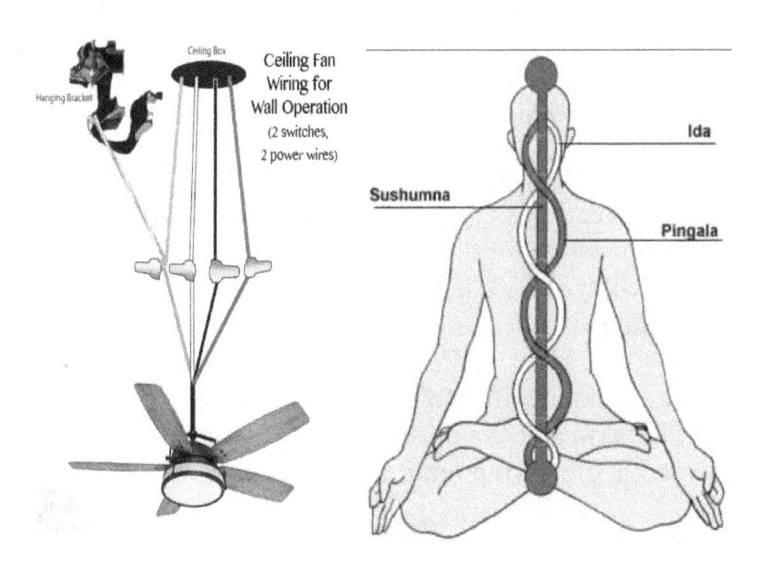

Nadis

Later this unit of electrical resistance was termed Ohm after Georg Ohm, a German physicist and mathematician. The symbol for Ohm coincidently is the symbol Ω Ohm or Ohm-mega (omega). This type of electrical resistance is related to how the chakras when aligned work in the body via the ida, pingala, sushumna and nadis.

One of the ways our bodies produce electricity is via the cerebral cortex and the pineal gland. The cerebral cortex covers the brain and is made of copper which mixes with carbon from the pineal gland to create electricity. The nervous system serves as the conduit to send the electricity down the body via nerves which are related to the nadis the principal energy channels. The pineal gland provides a masculine charge, and the pituitary gland a negative or feminine charge. These combined make the life force known in China as the Chi, Ki in Japan and in Prana in India. Christians will recognize this energy force as the Holy Spirit. This life force is like an electrical charge which causes life force energy to run up and down the spine the way electricity runs along a wire. The energy is divided into two like the AC/DC currents only one is masculine and one is feminine.

The energy charges the cerebral spinal fluid and is partly responsible for the spark that happens when the egg is fertilized by sperm. If the man retains the sperm via a practice known as trantric sex, it returns back up the spinal column to the brain and is known as shemen in the Hebrew language meaning the anointing oil. However, when he releases sperm and ejaculates it into the woman, it is known as semen, a life-giving force.

Shemen is the holy anointing oil as described in Exodus 30:22-25 and was created from:

כג וְאַתָּה קַח-לְךָ, בְּשָׂמִים רֹאשׁ, מָר-דְּרוֹר חֲמֵשׁ מֵאוֹת, וְקִנְּמָן-בֶּשֶׂם מַחֲצִיתוֹ חֲמִשִּׁים וּמָאתָיִם; וּקְנֵה-בֹשֶׂם, חֲמִשִּׁים וּמָאתָיִם.	23 'Take thou also unto thee the chief spices, of flowing myrrh five hundred shekels, and of sweet cinnamon half so much, even two hundred and fifty, and of sweet calamus two hundred and fifty,
כד וְקִדָּה, חֲמֵשׁ מֵאוֹת בְּשֶׁקֶל הַקֹּדֶשׁ; וְשֶׁמֶן זַיִת, הִין.	24 and of cassia five hundred, after the shekel of the sanctuary, and of olive oil a hin.
כה וְעָשִׂיתָ אֹתוֹ, שֶׁמֶן מִשְׁחַת-קֹדֶשׁ--רֹקַח מִרְקַחַת, מַעֲשֵׂה רֹקֵחַ; שֶׁמֶן מִשְׁחַת-קֹדֶשׁ, יִהְיֶה.	25 And thou shalt make it a holy anointing oil, a perfume compounded after the art of the perfumer; it shall be a holy anointing oil.
כו וּמָשַׁחְתָּ בוֹ, אֶת-אֹהֶל מוֹעֵד, וְאֵת, אֲרוֹן הָעֵדֻת.	26 And thou shalt anoint therewith the tent of meeting, and the ark of the testimony,

Olive oil or שמן זית *shemen zayit* in the Hebrew language shemen, sheh'-men; from H8080; שֶׁמֶן grease, especially liquid (as from the olive, often perfumed); figuratively, richness:—anointing, × fat (things), × fruitful, oil(-ed), ointment, olive, pine.
https://biblehub.com/str/hebrew/8081.htm

We find in Genesis 28:18, "And Jacob rose up early in the morning, and took the stone that he had put for his pillows, and set it up for a pillar, and poured oil upon the top of it. [19] And he called the name of that place Bethel: but the name of that city was called Luz at the first. Luz is a Hebrew word for "almond" which is an aphrodisiac.

Therefore, Jacob wrestled with Samael, the Angel of Lust & desire. Jacob then anoints the herm (stone) with שמן shemen. This Hebrew word is translated as "oil" and is a symbolic of how those who practice tantric sex transform their sexual energy, by "anointing their stone." Which symbolically is, the sexual oil that is not expelled from the body, but is transformed inside, to be carried up the spinal column via the sushumna and nadis - the pillar of stone - to the head, house of God (Beth El).

Notice this story relates to Genesis 32:30 where Jacob calls the place Peniel or Pineal which come from the word pine which is part of the description for Olive oil above. "Genesis 32: 30 "And Jacob called the name of the place Peniel: for I have seen God face to face, and my life is preserved." וַיִּקְרָא יַעֲקֹב שֵׁם הַמָּקוֹם, פְּנִיאֵל: כִּי-רָאִיתִי אֱלֹהִים פָּנִים אֶל-פָּנִים, וַתִּנָּצֵל נַפְשִׁי.

Thus, that tells the reader Bethel or the House of God and the Pineal are in the same area. There is a loose association of the word penis and pineal as is with shemen and semen. Chemically, sexual energy and the cerebral spinal fluid in the spinal column and around the brain are almost identical, they are very similar. They are a kind of salty fluid through which energies, forces move. One deals with the north pole (head/skull) and the other deals with the south pole (genital region). The Quran also speaks of this holy anointing oil in Surah Nuwr (the Light) [24.35] Allah is the light of the heavens and the earth; a likeness of His light is as a niche in which is a lamp, the lamp is in a glass, (and) the glass is as it were a brightly shining star, lit from a blessed olive-tree, neither eastern nor western, the oil whereof almost gives light though fire touch it not-- light upon light-- Allah guides to His light whom He pleases, and Allah sets forth parables for men, and Allah is Cognizant of all things.

اللَّهُ نُورُ السَّمَاوَاتِ وَالْأَرْضِ ۚ مَثَلُ نُورِهِ كَمِشْكَاةٍ فِيهَا مِصْبَاحٌ ۖ الْمِصْبَاحُ فِي زُجَاجَةٍ ۖ الزُّجَاجَةُ كَأَنَّهَا كَوْكَبٌ دُرِّيٌّ يُوقَدُ مِن شَجَرَةٍ مُّبَارَكَةٍ زَيْتُونَةٍ لَّا شَرْقِيَّةٍ وَلَا غَرْبِيَّةٍ يَكَادُ زَيْتُهَا يُضِيءُ وَلَوْ لَمْ تَمْسَسْهُ نَارٌ ۚ نُّورٌ عَلَىٰ نُورٍ ۗ يَهْدِي اللَّهُ لِنُورِهِ مَن يَشَاءُ ۚ وَيَضْرِبُ اللَّهُ الْأَمْثَالَ لِلنَّاسِ ۗ وَاللَّهُ بِكُلِّ شَيْءٍ عَلِيمٌ

To activate this anointing oil and align the chakras, one should meditate (fikr), chant (dhikr), pray (salat) and breathe properly to saturate the internal organs with oxygen.

When Muslims dhikr they are using the seven vowels found in the Arabic language. Vowels are very important to the ancient sciences of dhikr and in the ancient science of numerology called abjad in Arabic. Vowels relate to the soul path in numerology, in Pythagorean Numerology, each letter in your name is given a single digit number. The Soul Path Number expresses the deepest desires and inner workings of a person. It is what unconsciously motivates us day to day, and is the real you out of the three yous. There is the "you" you think you are, the "you" everyone perceives you to be, then there is the real you which is the soul path number. The heart's desire/soul path number is derived from the vowels (A, E, I, O, U ... and sometimes Y) of your full name at birth. These same vowel sounds are found in Arabic as well.

1 = FATHA = Short Vowel "A"

2 = DAMMAH = Short Vowel "O" or "U"

3 = KASRAH = Short Vowel "I" or "E"

4 = SOOKOOWN = Used for consonants lacking a vowel after them.

5= FATHATAIN= double FATHA (FATHA on the top of another FATHA)= FATHA + N= the short vowel "A"+ N: Ghad<u>an</u> = غدًا = Tomorrow

6= KASRATAIN= double KASRAH (KASRAH on the top of another KASRAH)= KASRAH+ N= the short vowel "i" or "e"+ N: Kurat<u>in</u>= كرةٍ =a ball

7= DAMMATAIN= double DAMMAH (DAMMAH next to another DAMMAH)= DAMMAH+ N= the short vowel "o" or "u"+ N: Kitab<u>un</u>= كتابٌ = **a** book

Qur'aanic Arabic Lessons for The Nubian Islaamic Hebrews (pgs 8a-9a), Nubian Islaamic Hebrews Ansaaru Allah Publication, Brooklyn, NY, 1986, As Sayyid Al Imaam Isa Al Haadi Al Mahdi

    The fathatain, kasratain and dammatain are not used as much as the fathah, kasrah, dammah and sookoown. Similarly, the higher spiritual chakras are not used as much as the lower four chakras.

    Several surahs in the Quran remind the Muslim to dhikr. Surahs 13:28, 18:24, and 33:41 are some examples. Surah 13:28. (Ar-Ra'd), "They are the ones whose hearts rejoice in remembering God. Absolutely, by remembering God, the hearts rejoice."

الَّذِينَ آمَنُوا وَتَطْمَئِنُّ قُلُوبُهُم بِذِكْرِ اللَّهِ ۗ أَلَا بِذِكْرِ اللَّهِ تَطْمَئِنُّ الْقُلُوبُ

Surah 18 (Al-Kahf), states a person who forgets to say, "God Willing," should immediately remember God by saying, "May my Lord guide me to do better next time." Surah 33 (Al-Ahzab), "O ye who believe! Celebrate the praises of Allah, and do this often,". Hadith state Muhammad said 'The best [dhikr] is *La ilaha illa'llah* ("there is no God but God"), and the best supplicatory prayer is *Al-hamdu li'llah* ("praise be to God")

Muslims believe dhikr is the best way to enter the higher levels of Heaven as the Sufis believe dhikr is a way to gain spiritual enlightenment and union with Allah. Declarations like *lā ilāha illa 'llāh*, "there is no god but God"; *Allāhu akbar,* "God is greatest"; *al-ḥamdu lī'llāh,* "praise be to God"; *astaghfiru 'llāh,* "I ask God's forgiveness"), repeated aloud or softly accompanied by proper posture and breathing will help. Another way to achieve this is via prayer or salaat. Muslims are obligated to pray at least five times a day based on the movement of the sun. The five obligatory prayers are fajr – the dawn prayer, dhuhr – noon prayer, asr – afternoon prayer, maghrib – sunset prayer and Isha'a the night prayer. At each prayer is a series of movements where different sayings are said at each movement. These movements are showing and named in the image below.

TAKBIR   AL-QIYYAM   RUKU   SUJUD   JULUS

Salaat

These movements are inexplicably similar to the movements in Yoga. According to Karima Burns, MH, ND who has a Doctorate in Naturopathy and a Masters in Herbal Healing states. *The Takbir and Al Qiyyam together are very similar to the Mountain Pose in yoga, which has been found to improve posture, balance, and self-awareness. This position also normalizes blood pressure and breathing, thus providing many benefits to asthma and heart patients.*

The placement of the hands on the chest during the Qiyyam position are said to activate the solar plexus " chakra," or nerve pathway, which directs our awareness of self in the world and controls the health of the muscular system, skin, intestines, liver, pancreas, gallbladder and eyes. When the hands are held open for du' a, they activate the heart "chakra," said to be the center of the feelings of love, harmony, and peace, and to control love and compassion. It also governs the health of the heart, lungs, thymus, immune system, and circulatory system.

Virtually all of the sounds of the Arabic language are uttered while reciting Qur' an, creating a balance in all affected areas of the body. Some specific sounds, in fact, correspond to major organs in the body. In his research and creation of eurhythmy, Rudolph Steiner (founder of the Waldorf Schools),, found that vibrations made when pronouncing the long vowels, 'A', 'E' and 'U,' stimulated the heart, lungs, and the thyroid, pineal, pituitary, and adrenal glands during laboratory tests.

The position of Ruku is very similar to the Forward Bend Position in yoga. Ruku stretches the muscles of the lower back, thighs, legs and calves, and allows blood to be pumped down into the upper torso. It tones the muscles of the stomach, abdomen, and kidneys. Forming a right angle allows the stomach muscles to develop, and prevents flabbiness in the mid-section.

This position also promotes a greater flow of blood into the upper regions of body - particularly to the head, eyes, ears, nose, brain, and lungs - allowing mental toxins to be released. Over time, this improves brain function and one's personality, and is an excellent stance to maintain the proper position of the fetus in pregnant women.

The Sujud is said to activate the "crown chakra," which is related to a person's spiritual connection with the universe around them and their enthusiasm for spiritual pursuits. This nerve pathway is also correlated to the health of the brain, nervous system, and pineal gland. Its healthy function balances ones interior and exterior energies. In Sujud, we also bend; thus activating the " base chakra," which controls basic human survival instincts and provides essential grounding. This helps to develop levelheaded and positive thinking along with a highly motivated view of life, and maintains the health of the lymph and skeletal systems, the prostate, bladder, and the adrenal glands. We also bend the "sacral chakra" during Sujud, thus benefiting and toning the reproductive organs.

The position of Al Qaadah, (or Julus) is similar to the Thunderbolt Pose in yoga, which firms the toes, knees, thighs, and legs. It is said to be good for those prone to excessive sleep, and those who like to keep long hours. Furthermore, this position assists in speedy digestion, aids the detoxification of the liver, and stimulates peristaltic action in the large intestine.

Last, but not least, the "throat chakra" is activated by turning the head towards first the right and then the left shoulder in the closing of the prayer. This nerve path is linked to the throat, neck, arms, hands, bronchial, and hearing - effecting individual creativity and communication. It is believed that a person who activates all seven nerve pathways at least once a day can remain well balanced emotionally, physically and spiritually. Since this is the goal of all sincere Muslims, we all should strive to attain the perfection of stance, recitation, and breathing recommended in the Hadith while performing our prayers - the very same techniques of perfection taught in popular yoga, Tai Chi, and many other exercise classes."
http://www.fuccha.in/namaaz-yoga-of-islamic-prayer-and-its-medical-benefits

Yoga Vs Salaat Positions

HOW TO PRAY (SALAT)

First Rak'ah | Second Rak'ah

Yoga/Salaat

ALLAH, THE QURAN, VENUS AND YOU

The western world is just now coming into knowledge of these things; therefore, this simple exercise is given to assist if the reader is interested in trying these techniques for help with aligning and tuning the chakras. The chanting creates the vibrations and our greatest vibrational instrument is our own body. To begin this exercise, the novice should sit alone preferably in the dark and take deep breaths to relax remembering to breath in through the nostrils and exhaling out of the mouth.

Breaths should be deep and fill the stomach while keeping the chest still. Proper breathing should not involve chest movements. Watching a new born baby breathe will show you how one should breath. There are various ways to align the chakra or heal the area of the body that overlays the chakra. Chanting is one of the more effective ways. If one is wanting a total alignment start with the root chakra and ascend to the crown chakra. Again, take a deep breath and exhale while saying the tone of "uh" as in Tut for the root chakra and visualize that part of the body being aligned or healed. Say each tone three to nine times. Visualize in the mind's eye the corresponding color to the chakra you are aligning.

You can also visualize all chakras being aligned one by one clearing blockages. Chanting in rhythms and tones gives frequencies that help heal the body. Dr. Royal R. Rife, M.D. (1888-1971) conducted research with a machine he developed called a "frequency generator" that applies currents of specific frequencies to the body. He concluded that every disease has a specific frequency. His research demonstrated that certain frequencies could prevent the development of disease, and that others would neutralize disease. Since we do not have access to this machine, we have other natural devices that produce the same results. In ancient times they used a lyre which is a seven stringed musical instrument much like a harp.

Egyptian Women playing harp

The Egyptian woman on the right is playing a lyre and the one on the left is -playing a harp. In the bible, a harp was used to remove the body of negative energy or spirits. 1 Samuel 16: [23] "And it came to pass, when the evil spirit from God was upon Saul, that David took a harp, and played with his hand: so Saul was refreshed, and was well, and the evil spirit departed from him."

וְהָיָה, בִּהְיוֹת רוּחַ-אֱלֹהִים אֶל-שָׁאוּל, וְלָקַח דָּוִד אֶת-הַכִּנּוֹר וְנִגֵּן בְּיָדוֹ; וְרָוַח לְשָׁאוּל וְטוֹב לוֹ, וְסָרָה מֵעָלָיו רוּחַ הָרָעָה.

The harp became the basis of the piano, as the piano is merely a horizontal harp. The seven strings on the lyre was related to the seven planets and each planet has a vibration of the seven vowels which became the basis for an octave in music. Just as the piano with its 88 keys relate to the 88 constellations recognized by NASA. Music is the healing force of the world – O'Jays.

Planet	Color	Musical Note	Musical Scale
Moon	Orange	G Sharp / A Flat	Fa
Mercury	Yellow	E	Mi
Venus	Green	F Sharp / G Flat	La
Sun	Gold	C	Do
Mars	Red	C	So
Jupiter	Indigo (blue violet)	A Sharp / B Flat	Ti
Saturn	Violet	A	Re

Music Chart

Make Lifestyle Choices Based on Understanding of Energy Frequencies

Here are 5 essential tips:

1. Cook your meals with fresh ingredients and garden herbs. Fresh produce has a frequency up to 15 MHz, dry herbs from 12 to 22 MHz, and fresh herbs from 20 to 27 MHz. Avoid processed and canned foods since they have no measurable frequency whatsoever.

2. Go offline and reduce your usage of electronic devices periodically. You are probably aware about the ill effects of electronic devices but continue to use them anyway. Here is why it is important to go on an electronic fast. Your lamps, television, radio, phone, microwave and all emit dissonant energies. According to **David Stewart** in The Chemistry of Essential Oils Made Simple, *when something vibrates at many dissonant frequencies, it produces "chaotic or incoherent frequencies." They fracture the human electrical field and result in illness and diseases.*

3. Avoid drugs and products that contain toxic ingredients. Pharmaceuticals and synthetic oils are substances that also do not produce coherent frequencies.

4. Apply therapeutic grade essential oils. Most naturally occurring substances –including essential oils – have coherent frequencies that resonate harmoniously with the electrical field of the human body. *Thus, by applying an essential oil, you can restore your body back to its original natural harmonic resonance.* For an oil blend, its therapeutic frequency is derived from the combination of single oils. Disease or illness either doesn't manifest or is resolved.

5. Use the power of intention. Amplify the effect of essential oils with the power of positive intention such as prayer! *Prayer raises your energy frequency by 15MHz. https://aromawealth.com/raise-your-energy-frequency-with-essential-oils/*

As one starts the process of proper breathing and meditation their brain waves will begin to go through different phases. The four brain waves in order of highest frequency to lowest are as follows: beta (26), alpha (14), theta (8), and delta (4) for a total of 52. Beta deals with conscious thought and encompasses mundane duties throughout the day including stress and the inability to relax on the negative side but on the positive side it deals with memory and problem solving. Alpha waves are more in tuned with day dreaming and at times being too relaxed as positives but anxiety and OCD on the negative side. Theta waves brings us anxiety and stress on the negative pole but intuition and creativity on the positive poles. Lastly Delta which has ADHD and the inability to think as negatives but natural healing and deep sleep as positives.

As one mediates, the brain waves begin to slow down and allows the body to reach higher states of consciousness because useless thoughts and actions are stifled. The stillness and solitude brings a peaceful and tranquil environment that allows the mind to expand etherically to make contact with the divine.

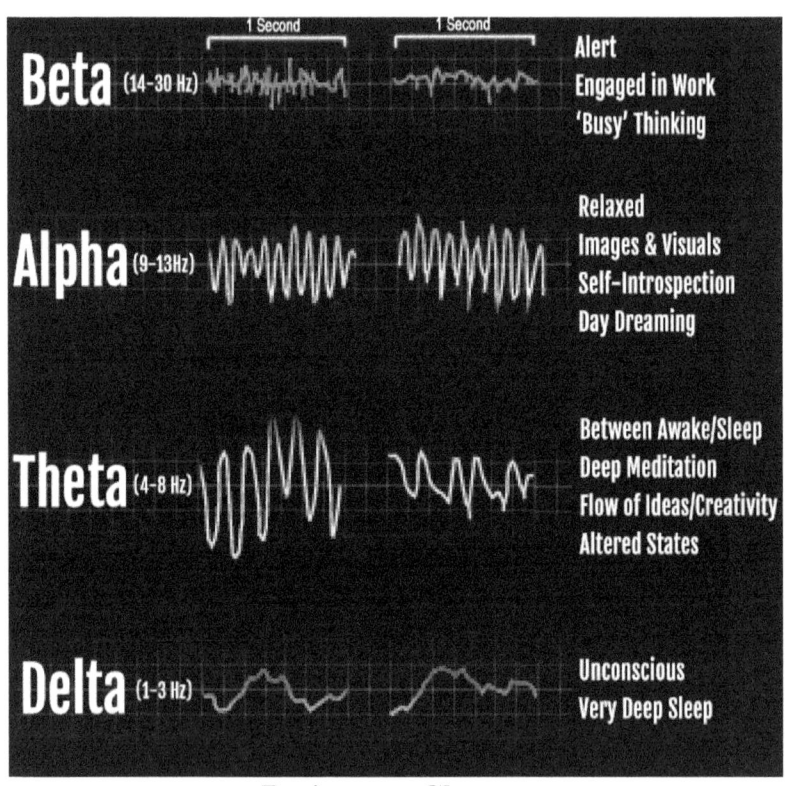

Brain wave Chart

VENUS – MARS

"Allat was the feminine version of Allah, so was Baalat the feminine version of Baal. Al-Uzza ('the mighty') represented the Virgin warrior facet; she was a desert Goddess of the morning star who had a sanctuary in a grove of acacia trees to the south of Mecca, where she was worshipped in the form of a sacred stone. Al-Lat, whose name means simply 'Goddess', was the Mother facet connected with the Earth and its fruits and the ruler of fecundity. She was worshipped at At-Ta'if near Mecca in the form of a great uncut block of white granite. Manat, the crone facet of the Goddess, ruled fate and death. Her principal sanctuary was located on the road between Mecca and Medina, where she was worshipped in the form of a black uncut stone.

One of the aspects of goddess worship that has survived in Islam, as well as, for example, in Roman Catholicism, is the rosary. Through the ages the worshippers of goddesses had used the rosary for prayers and it is still in use in the worship of female deities all over the world, for example by Hindus in India. The rosary is connected with fertility worship when the deity's name is repeated over and over again. (Compare to Matthew 6:7-13 and Acts 19:34.) It is called tasbih or subha in Arabic, and simply means 'an object which one praises.' The Muslim rosary is supposed to contain 99 beads, representing the titles of 'Allah', but usually it only has 33 beads, slipped through one's fingers three times. (Compare to the Koran 7:180.) This pagan custom, which is dated to Astarte worship from about 800 BCE, still survives in Islam as well as in many other cults around the world." (McLean, The Triple Goddess, 80.) The Triple Goddess: An Exploration of the Archetypal Feminine (Hermetic Research Series) Paperback – June 1, 1989 by Adam McLean.

Isis had the same basic name as the Arabic *Al-'Uzza*, the Sublime One, the name of Venus/Ishtar. All virgin deities who later became pregnant and birthed a savior God. Allah is short for El and one of El's elongated versions is Ayil meaning Ram according to Strong's concordance. " 'ayil, ah'-yil; from the same as H193; properly, strength; hence, anything strong; specifically a chief (politically); also a ram (from his strength); a pilaster (as a strong support); an oak or other strong tree:—mighty (man), lintel, oak, post, ram, tree."
http://www.eliyah.com/cgi-bin/strongs.cgi?file=hebrewlexicon&isindex=193

The ram will show up in the most interesting of places, for instance, in Ancient Egypt there is a deity named Amun Ra who is a ram headed deity. It is from this deity's name that we get the word Amen used at the end of prayers. Other places it has appeared is in the name of Rachel wife of Jacob, the son of Isaac who is the son of Abraham. Rachel fem. Proper name, biblical daughter of Laban and wife of Jacob, from Late Latin, form Greek Rhakhel, form Hebrew Rahel, literally "ewe" (compare Arabic rahil, Aramaic rahla, Akkadian lahru, a metathesized form). Or a female ram called sheep. These hidden messages were not designed for the novice reader and practitioner of religion. It is designed for those who truly seek the knowledge of the mysteries of the ancients which is the study of the stars. Astrologically this was during the time of the Age of Aries which was approximately 4,320 years ago.

The official name for sheep is Ovis Aries in Latin
one word sounds like
the word ovaries is from
us meaning egg-keeper or
. The eggs are kept in the
uterus or Uterus (Taurus).
Uterus is from Latin
uterus meaning womb,
belly. In Egypt the cow or
bull-headed deity was
Hat-Heru also called
Hathor who the Greeks
identified with Aphrodite. She is the daughter of Ra or Amun Ra. It is from this deity the Quran gets its longest Surah called Baqarah. Hat-Heru is the Egyptian Goddess of Love, Beauty and Protection. Coincidently the most famous verse in the Quran is found in Surah Baqarah and is called the Throne Verse and is said by Muslim when traveling to give them protection. She would incorporate the age of Taurus approximately 6,480 years ago and signifies why ancient cultures had bull/cow deities. Inclusive of the Hindus who made cows sacred after the Goddess Nandini whose name means Daughter in Sanskrit. The authors of *The Quick and the Dead* believe the ankh, djed, and waas symbols are rooted in "cattle culture", with the ankh representing the thoracic vertebra of a bull (seen in cross section), the djed the base or sacrum of a bull's spine, and the waas a staff (*Gordon, Andrew Hunt; Schwabe, Calvin W (2004). The Quick and the Dead: Biomedical Theory in Ancient Egypt First Edition. Brill/Styx. ISBN 90-04-12391-1.*)

Aries the first of the zodiac signs and means "to butt" is closely related to the Greek God Ares meaning injurer, destroyer and is associated with the Roman war God, Mars. Whereas Taurus is associated with the female deity Hat-

Heru who is known by other names in various cultures. These dualities of the zodiac ages were secretly hidden in the Holy Bible as Cain and Abel. Abel was keeper of the sheep aka Aries and Cain was a tiller of the ground or Taurus as cows were used to plow the earth. According to Genesis 4:**2** "And she again bare his brother Abel. And Abel was a keeper of sheep, but Cain was a tiller of the ground." Furthermore, in the elements of Astrology, Taurus is an earth sign.

וַתֹּסֶף לָלֶדֶת, אֶת-אָחִיו אֶת-הָבֶל; וַיְהִי-הֶבֶל, רֹעֵה צֹאן, וְקַיִן, הָיָה עֹבֵד אֲדָמָה

      This duality of both a masculine deity and a feminine deity is also found hidden within the pages of the Quran. Secretly hidden within the Quran is the rotation of the planets Mars (Allah) and Venus (Allat). The Quran also talks about the rotation of the Earth. Dr. Haluk Nurbaki states "You see the mountains and think them jamid (lifeless, motionless); yet they progress, just as clouds progress. Such is the handiwork of God, who has disposed of everything in firmness. He is completely aware of all you do." Verses from the Glorious Koran and the Facts of Science, author Dr. Haluk Nurbaki 1989, Ankara, Turkey, This is taken from the Quran Surah 27.88 the Ant. The planets Venus and Mars are the Roman names of the planets found in the Quran. In Arabic, the names are different for Venus, Mars and the other celestial bodies in our solar system. Yet because the Quran has Roman Catholic influence, the Roman names were inserted into the Quran. Although the Quran states it was sent down in the Arabic language, you find words from other languages in the Quran. Surah Ta-Ha [20.113] And thus have We sent it down an Arabic Quran.

وَكَذَلِكَ أَنْزَلْنَاهُ قُرْآنًا عَرَبِيًّا وَصَرَّفْنَا فِيهِ مِنَ الْوَعِيدِ لَعَلَّهُمْ يَتَّقُونَ أَوْ يُحْدِثُ لَهُمْ ذِكْرًا

ALLAH, THE QURAN, VENUS AND YOU

The name Venus (*Waaw-Alif-Nuun-Alif-Shiin* in Arabic) appear side by side in Surah Anfal (8) aya 72. The next sequence of letters spelling out the word Venus in Arabic appears Surah Hud (11) ayat 3. There are 243 verses between these two surahs. Venus takes 225 Earth days to revolve around the sun and 243 Earth days to rotate on its axis. Coincidently it takes Venus exactly 243 days to revolve on its own axis. The same thing happens with the masculine planet Mars. The letters that comprise the word Mars (*Miim-Alif-Raa-Shiin* in Arabic) first appear side by side in Surah Mu'minuwn (23) ayat 44. Mars next appears in verse 45. In other words, Mars appear just **1** verse later. It takes the planet Mars just 1 day to revolve around its own axis. The letters comprising the word Venus appear side by side from right to left in verse 72 of Surat al-Anfal. Additionally, the letters comprising the word Venus appear side by side from right to left in verse or ayyat 3 in Surah Hud.

VENUS

Venus in Arabic   **Surah Al Anfal**   **Surah Hud**

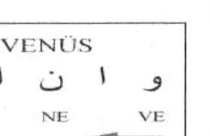

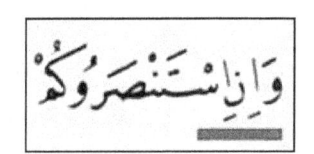

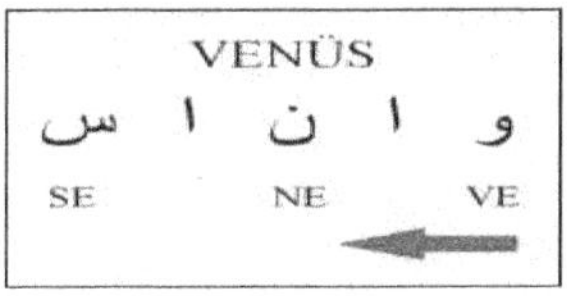

MARS

Mars in Arabic   **Surah Mu'minuwn**   **Surah Mu'minuwn**

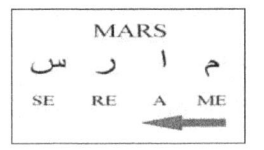

The letters comprising the word Mars appear side by side from right to left in verse 44 of Surat al-Mu'minun. The letters comprising the word Mars appear side by side from right to left in verse 45 of Surat al-Mu'minun. The duality of Venus/Mars is also represented in Greek cosmology as Aphrodite, the goddess of love and Ares, the god of war. The writers of the Quran understood this cosmology was taken from earlier cosmologies especially that of Africans. The hidden science of measurements, rotations and the likes were incorporated into the building of the Giza plateau in Cairo.   Cairo's official name is Al Qahirah in the Arabic language (القاهرة) which means the place or camp of Mars. This is because Mars was rising when Cairo was being founded. Thus, it is no surprise to see the scale of the planets Venus, Earth and Mars matches the scale of the pyramids. Venus to the Khaf Re pyramid, Khufu (Ra Ufu) to Earth and Men Ka Re to Mars.

Planets/Pyramids

Another aspect of the Mars/Venus dichotomy is found in the book of Genesis in 2:5 "And every plant of the field before it was in the earth, and every herb of the field before it grew: for the LORD God had not caused it to rain upon the earth, and there was not a man to till the ground."

וְכֹל שִׂיחַ הַשָּׂדֶה, טֶרֶם יִהְיֶה בָאָרֶץ, וְכָל-עֵשֶׂב הַשָּׂדֶה, טֶרֶם יִצְמָח: כִּי לֹא הִמְטִיר יְהוָה אֱלֹהִים, עַל-הָאָרֶץ, וְאָדָם אַיִן, לַעֲבֹד אֶת-הָאֲדָמָה

Where it states literally that God had not made a man to break the soil so that seeds can be planted. However, this is not the real meaning, because in Genesis 1:11 there was already trees/plants with fruit Genesis 1:11 And God said, Let the earth bring forth grass, the herb yielding seed, and the fruit tree yielding fruit after his kind, whose seed is in itself, upon the earth: and it was so. So, this verse in Genesis 2:5 is not talking about husbandry in the literally sense. It is referring to reproduction.

The ground is the word Adamah אֲדָמָה in Hebrew and is a feminine noun whereas the word Adam אָדָם in

verse 5 is a masculine noun. The "ah" at the end of the word Adam makes it a feminine word. This is saying there were women on the planet but there was no man to fertilize or have intercourse with the women.

ISLAM and ASTROLOGY

According to author Rom Landau who states "At the time of Muhammad, however, he was on the ascendancy. He had replaced the moon god as lord of the Ka'aba although still relegated to an inferior position below various tribal idols and three powerful goddesses: al-Manat, goddess of fate, al-Lat, mother of the gods, and al-Uzza, the planet Venus." (Islam and the Arabs, Rom Landau, 1958 p 11-21)

Venus' relationship to the religion of Islam is incorporated in all facets of the Arabian religion. For instance, Islam is called the religion of peace Surah Baqarah 2:11 "And when it is said to them, Do not make mischief in the land, they say: We are but peace-makers."

وَإِذَا قِيلَ لَهُمْ لَا تُفْسِدُوا فِي الْأَرْضِ قَالُوا إِنَّمَا نَحْنُ مُصْلِحُونَ

A similar passage is found in the bible in the book of Matthew. Matthew 5:9 "Blessed are the peacemakers: for they shall be called the children of God." Venus energy is harmonious, and this is why people with Venus prominent in their natal charts are often seen as peace-makers. A natal chart is a chart of the sky that shows where the planets were at your exact time and place of birth.

The first surah, Arabic for Chapter, in the Quran is Al Fatihah which means the Opening. It was not the first surah revealed but it is chronologically first in the Quran. Yet, Venus' sacred month is April which comes from the Roman etymologists and is understood to mean "to open" from the word aperire. The reader should see the correspondence with Al Fatihah meaning opening and April meaning to open. It is related to the ancient Egyptian deity Ptah whose name means opener.

	afro-asiatique *piṭaḥ « ouvrir »	
↙	↓	↘
arabe /fataḥ/	égyptien *pth*	hébreu פתח /pathaḥ/
↓	↓	
Fatiha Fatah	Egypte	

بِسْمِ اللَّهِ الرَّحْمَٰنِ الرَّحِيمِ ۝
ٱلْحَمْدُ لِلَّهِ رَبِّ ٱلْعَٰلَمِينَ ۝ ٱلرَّحْمَٰنِ
ٱلرَّحِيمِ ۝ مَٰلِكِ يَوْمِ ٱلدِّينِ ۝
إِيَّاكَ نَعْبُدُ وَإِيَّاكَ نَسْتَعِينُ ۝
ٱهْدِنَا ٱلصِّرَٰطَ ٱلْمُسْتَقِيمَ ۝ صِرَٰطَ
ٱلَّذِينَ أَنْعَمْتَ عَلَيْهِمْ غَيْرِ
ٱلْمَغْضُوبِ عَلَيْهِمْ وَلَا ٱلضَّآلِّينَ ۝

Al- Fatihah

1. In the name of God, Most Gracious, Most Merciful.
2. Praise be to God, The Cherisher and Sustainer of the Worlds.
3. Most Gracious, Most Merciful.
4. Master of the Day of Judgment.
5. Thee do we worship, And Thine aid we seek.
6. Show us the straight way,
7. The way of those on whom, Thou hast bestowed Thy Grace, Is not wrath, And who go not astray.

Al Fatihah

ALLAH, THE QURAN, VENUS AND YOU

The holiest day of the week in Islam is Friday called in Arabic, Jummah. Surah 62:9 Al Jummah - The Congregation "O you who believe! when the call is made for prayer on Friday, then hasten to the remembrance of Allah and leave off trading; that is better for you, if you know."

يَا أَيُّهَا الَّذِينَ آمَنُوا إِذَا نُودِيَ لِلصَّلَاةِ مِن يَوْمِ الْجُمُعَةِ فَاسْعَوْا إِلَىٰ ذِكْرِ اللَّهِ وَذَرُوا الْبَيْعَ ۚ ذَٰلِكُمْ خَيْرٌ لَّكُمْ إِن كُنتُمْ تَعْلَمُونَ

Jummah is the sixth day of the week. The word Jummah or *al Jumu'ah* is derived from *jama'a-yajma'u-jaman* as its root, means to gather, to collect, to unite, to count, and to combine. The meaning of Jummah itself is unity, friendship, harmony (*al ulfah*), and meeting (*al ijtima*). Coincidently, Venus is associated with Friday as the day of Venus, Friday takes its name from Frigga, the Goddess of Love and Transformation. The word "frigg" is connected to sex, as is Venus/venereal. Her other name is Aphrodite/aphrodisiac. The Greek equivalent of Venus is Aphrodite who metamorphosed herself into a fish, which animal was considered to possess the greatest generative powers. Many words within the English language are related to reproduction we just were not aware of their etymologies.

Orchid - 1845, introduced by John Lindley in "School Botanty," from Modern Latin Orchideæ (Linnaeus), the plant's family name, from Latin orchis, a kind of orchid, from Greek orkhis (genitive orkheos) "orchid," literally "testicle," from PIE *h(o)rghi-, the standard IE word for "testicle" (source also of Avestan erezi, Armenian orjik' "testicles," Old Irish uirge, Hittite arki- "testicle," Lithuanian eržilas "stallion").
https://www.etymonline.com/word/orchid#etymonline_v_7 121

Vanilla - During Hernando Cortes' conquest of the Aztec empire, his men discovered the vanilla plant and dubbed it *vainilla*, literally "little pod" or "little sheath," from the Latin *vagina*, "sheath."
https://www.etymonline.com/word/vanilla#etymonline_v_4632

Vagina - "sexual passage of the female from the vulva to the uterus," 1680s, medical Latin, from specialized use of Latin vagina "sheath, scabbard, covering; sheath of an ear of grain, hull, husk" (plural vaginae), a word of uncertain origin.
https://www.etymonline.com/word/vagina#etymonline_v_4600

Seminar - Seminar" comes from the Latin seminarium, meaning "breeding ground" or "plant nursery," which itself comes from the Latin *seminarius*, meaning "of seed." Given the words' phonological likeness, it's pretty obvious that they all come down to the Latin *semen*, "seed."

https://www.etymonline.com/word/seminar#etymonline_v_23190

Avocado - yet another generation that looked at plants and saw balls, 18th-century Spaniards took the vegetable fruit's name from an earlier Spanish version, *aquacate*, which evolved from the region's pre-conquest Nahuatl *ahuakati*, meaning "testicle."
https://www.etymonline.com/word/avocado#etymonline_v_19006

Gwen - Proto-Indo-European root meaning "woman." It forms all or part of: androgynous; banshee; gynarchy; gyneco-; gynecology; gynecomastia; gyno-; misogyny; polygyny; quean; queen. It is the hypothetical source

of/evidence for its existence is provided by: Sanskrit janis "a woman," gná "wife of a god, a goddess;" Avestan jainish "wife;" Armenian kin "woman;" Greek gyné "a woman, a wife;" Old Church Slavonic zena, Old Prussian genna "woman;" Gaelic bean "woman;" Old English cwen "queen, female ruler of a state, woman, wife;" Gothic qino "a woman, wife, qéns "queen."
https://www.etymonline.com/word/*gwen-#etymonline_v_52790

    As stated earlier, the Quraysh tribe uses a fish as it's symbol and on Friday's most Catholics eat fish, a fertility symbol. Venus is connected with beauty, sex and love and the feminine! This is why you can get the word venereal disease...from Venus.

    FAJR is the pre-dawn pray that coincides with the sun rise, just as Venus is the bright morning star that coincides with sun rise. During its 225-day orbit around the sun Venus makes 5 conjunctions. The 360-degree orbit plus the five conjunctions equates to 360/5 or the sacred number 72, the number of virgins in paradise for the Islamic faithful believing men. One must note here, that since the Ka'aba was initially dedicated to Allat a so-called moon deity, it has specific female artifacts still incorporated into its building. Ka'aba is an Arabic word meaning cube. The Ka'aba is a six-sided black building, each side is 360 degrees. Therefore, 360 degrees multiplied by 6 is 2,160 degrees. This coincides with the diameter of the moon which is 2,160 miles. The guardians of the most holy shrine in Islam called the Ka'aba in Mecca are called Bani Shaybah,or sons of the old woman. In the northeast corner of the Ka'aba is a black (brown) meteorite called the black stone. The stone was also called Kubaba, Kuba or Kube, and has been linked with the name of Cybele (Kybela), the Great Mother of the Gods. The black stone is shaped like the female sexual organ or yoni. Yawn (Yoni) - 1300, yenen, yonen, from Old English ginian, gionian "open the mouth wide, yawn, gape," from Proto-Germanic *gin- (source also of Old Norse gina "to yawn," Dutch geeuwen, Old High German ginen, German gähnen "to yawn"), from PIE *ghai- "to yawn, gape" (source also of Old Church Slavonic zijajo "to gape, https://www.etymonline.com/word/yawn#etymonline_v_44484

Ka'aba/Black Stone

When Muslims go to Mecca as one of their five obligatory requirements, they make what is known as Hajj, an annual pilgrimage to the Kaaba to kiss the black stone. This pilgrimage is similar to the Catholics pilgrimage to Rome to kiss and touch the feet of St. Peter. Since Catholicism existed before Islam, it is obvious that this tradition actually comes from the Catholics.

ALLAH, THE QURAN, VENUS AND YOU

Kissing the feet of St. Peter/Kissing Black Stone

Yet, I'm sure you are wondering why the feet of St. Peter? Earlier you read that all Catholic cardinals and popes learn astrology. Well, Peter is synonymous with Jupiter (Ju Piter or the Jew, Peter, taken from the Egyptian deity Ptah pronounced Pe Tah). In astrology Jupiter and Neptune rules Pisces and Pisces rules the feet in medical astrology also known as iatromatematics.

Annually, around the Easter holiday the Pope washes and kisses the feet of believers on Holy Thursday Mass. (Jupiter rules Thursday and the number 3 like Venus rules Friday and the number 6) The Gospel recounts Jesus washing the feet of his own disciples John 13: [14] If I then, your Lord and Master, have washed your feet; ye also ought to wash one another's feet. In another instance Mary Magdalene washed the feet of Jesus with her hair and a special ointment called Spikenard or Nard that serves as an aphrodisiac. John 12:3 Then took Mary a pound of ointment of spikenard, very costly, and anointed the feet of Jesus, and wiped his feet with her hair: and the house was filled with the odor of the ointment. Pisces is two fish hence the association with the two feet. When looking at the Yoni it is a shaped like a sacred geometry symbol called the Vesica Piscis. The Vesica Piscis is the shape made when two circles are joined together at their vertices. This symbol is throughout the ancient as well as modern world. In the modern world is seen at the base of the Washington monument in Banneker City misnomer Washington, D.C. and it encircles the Washington monument, yet you can only see this from an aerial view.

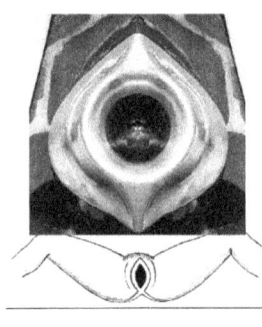

Vesica Piscis

Vesica Piscis

    Also, inside of the Kaaba are three pillars and each is designated for the three female goddesses called Allat, Al Uzza and Manat mentioned in the Quran. Surah 53: 19] Have you then considered the Lat and the Uzza,[53.20] And Manat, the third, the last? وَمَنَاةَ الثَّالِثَةَ الْأُخْرَىٰ

Pillars in Ka'aba

ALLAH, THE QURAN, VENUS AND YOU

Tomb of Muhammad

The Vesica piscis is proximately displayed at the Nation's capital at the Washington monument when view aerially. Take note how the Washington monument and the Capitol building resemble the tomb of Muhammad with the dome (Capitol building) and the minaret (Washington monument). These are fertility symbols and shows the duality of masculine/feminine principles. The Capitol building houses the Unite States Congress which has the House of Representatives and the Senate. House of Representatives United States (HORUS).

The Washington monument is the phallus and the Vesica piscis would be the womb/yoni. What is not widely known is when Washington D.C. or Bannaker City was founded Sirius was on the eastern horizon. The two circles that form the Vesica Piscis engulfing the Washington monument are the rotation of Sirius A and Sirius B. Sirius A & B were identified by the Dogon tribe of West Africa long before Europeans telescopes were created. In the Dogon tradition, every 60 years, the earth, the sun and Sirius are aligned and is called Sigui.

Sirius is called Sigui Tolo by the Dogons. The Washington monument would represent Sigui Tolo as it was on the horizon when the Washington monument was being constructed on July 4, 1848.

On America's Independence Day, Sirius is usually due east in the 13th degree of Cancer. This accounts for why there were 13 original colonies.

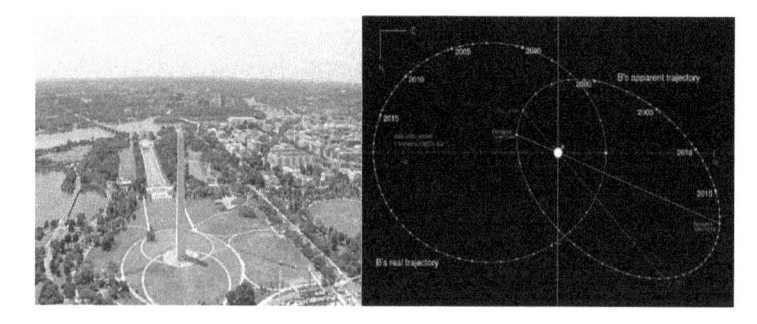

Sirius A/B rotation

Muslims love to tell non-Muslims their Prophet is the seal of all the prophets. What they fail to realize is this is symbolic as well. The bible speaks of the seven seals found on the backside. Revelations 5:1 And I saw in the right hand of him that sat on the throne a book written within and on the backside, sealed with seven seals. This is speaking of the seven chakras. Therefore, when you read in Surah 33 ayyat 40 in part "but (he is) the messenger of Allah and the seal of the prophets". This is of course symbolic of the seven prophets or seven seals. Notice in the image how David whose name means beloved is the heart chakra which resembles the Six-pointed star. Adam whose name means red represents the root chakra associated with earth. Adam was created from the black mud/earth according to Surah 17 of the Quran. Musa/Moses who had a speech impediment is the throat chakra.

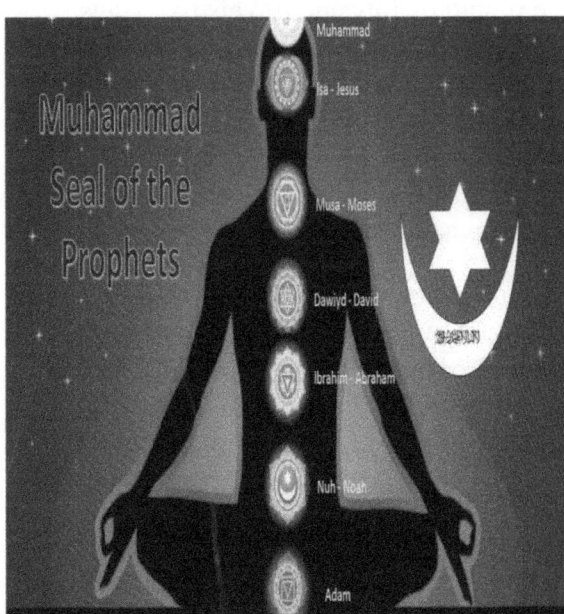

Abraham/Ibrahim represents the solar plexus because he was from Ur of Chaldea. Ur is fire. Abraham was the first Hebrew or Heb Heru a priest of light.

Nuh/Noah is the navel chakra, from where we get the word Navy which deals with water which directly implies the flood. In astrology the constellation Cancer deals with water as it is cardinal water. Noah's story is as astrological as they come. It deals with the sun as it reaches Cancer during the month of July and travels five signs down to Sagittarius which begins in November. Accordingly, the time he started building the ark to the time it rested is roughly 150 days or five zodiac months. Known as JASON for July, August, September, October and November. If you look at the decan of Cancer, it had a star cluster called Argo Navis meaning the boat.

Similarly, Greeks have a story called Jason and the Argonauts who were looking for the golden fleece. Argonauts meaning C16: from Greek *Argonautēs,* from *Argō* the name of Jason's ship + *nautēs* sailor]. https://www.etymonline.com/word/Argonaut#etymonline_v_26507

This is also where we get the word nautical dealing with water; seamen of which Noah and he sons were seamen. The shorten version of the story of Noah is told in the Quran in Surah 71 entitled Nuh. However, a more detailed version of the story of Noah is found in Genesis 6 of the bible. We are told Noah was told to build a boat (Argo Navis) and to take two of every animal into the ark. Thus, when we return to the constellations, we find two bears (Usra Major and Ursa Minor) in the Gemini decan, two donkeys (Asellus Australis and Asellus Borealis) in the cancer decan, two dogs (Canis Major and Canis Minor) in Gemini, and two lions near the Leo constellation. Once the Ark is closed for the 40 days and 40 nights, this relates to the total time the planet Venus is in retrograde. Next, Noah sends a raven to seek dry land, the Raven is the constellation Corvus which is found in Leo/Virgo. Corvus comes from the Latin word (genitive *Corvi*), literally, raven. Next in Genesis 8:11 Noah sends a dove out who returns with a tree branch. This is the constellation Columba which is a late Latin word meaning dove. This constellation is situated between Taurus and Gemini. In older constellation maps it was drawn with an olive branch in its beak. This entire story was taken from the ancient Egyptian Boat of the Ra or the Bark of Ra meaning boat of the Sun. Later it was called the Bark of Khonsu the moon deity. Which makes it the Boat of the Moon known to you as in Spanish as Barca De Luna or Barcelona a word with both masculine (barco) and feminine (luna) words. The Spanish language has an abundance of Arabic words in it and more than likely comes from the Moors civilizing the Spanish people in 717 A.D.

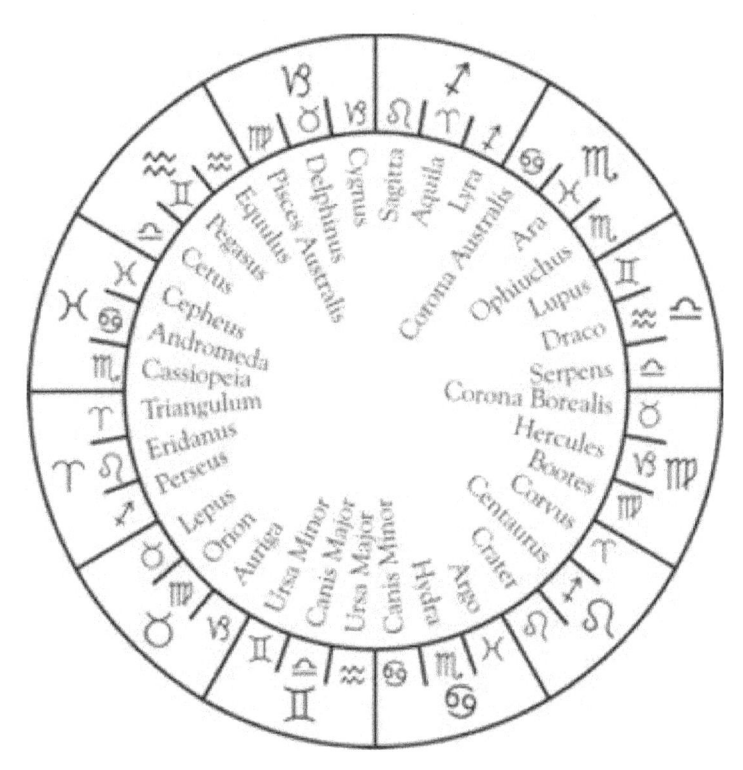

Zodiac calendar

As we see, each chakra represents one of the major prophets in Islam, so too do these prophets represent other aspects of spirituality or consciousness. Ancient Greek philosophers concluded there were five different levels of consciousness. According to Greek philosophers, these five stages are earth, water, air, fire and spirit. Symbolically represented in the Bible and Quran as Earth – Adam, Water – Noah, Air – Jesus, Fire – Muhammad and Spirit – the Messiah. Adam was the first man made of earth. After the Earth was destroyed by Water the new Adam was Noah. Later, Jesus was the new Adam and became Fire; he foretold of the Holy Spirit or comforter who is Air or the age of Aquarius the signed associated with Air. Jesus said when the holy spirit or comforter comes, he will glorify me which is what the Quran does, it glorifies Jesus. "I will ask the Father, and He will give you another Counselor to be with you forever" (John 14:16). Thus, you can plainly see how each "Adam" was a representation of the five stages of consciousness.

Five levels of consciousness

ALLAH, THE QURAN, VENUS AND YOU

The Quran has some outright and some subtleties showing its connection to astrology and astronomy. For example, it has Surahs dedicated to the Sun (Surah 91), Moon (Surah 54), Stars (Surah 53) and constellations (Surah 85). The Quran tells its followers to stars at night. Surah [6.97] "And He it is Who has made the stars for you that you might follow the right way thereby in the darkness of the land and the sea; truly We have made plain the communications for a people who know." وَهُوَ الَّذِي جَعَلَ لَكُمُ النُّجُومَ لِتَهْتَدُوا بِهَا فِي ظُلُمَاتِ الْبَرِّ وَالْبَحْرِ ۗ قَدْ فَصَّلْنَا الْآيَاتِ لِقَوْمٍ يَعْلَمُونَ

Also, in Surah [16.16] And landmarks; and by the stars they find the right way. Like the Holy Bible, the Quran says the Sun, Moon and Stars are for signs. Surah [16.12] "And He has made subservient for you the night and the day and the sun and the moon, and the stars are made subservient by His commandment; most surely there are signs in this for a people who ponder."

وَسَخَّرَ لَكُمُ اللَّيْلَ وَالنَّهَارَ وَالشَّمْسَ وَالْقَمَرَ ۖ وَالنُّجُومُ مُسَخَّرَاتٌ بِأَمْرِهِ ۗ إِنَّ فِي ذَٰلِكَ لَآيَاتٍ لِقَوْمٍ يَعْقِلُونَ

However, there are the not so direct references as well. For example, the largest Surah in the Quran is Surah Baqarah and it means the Cow. Surah Baqarah is representative of the Taurus constellation. It's almost as if the Quran was following the first three signs of the Zodiac beginning with Fatihah meaning opening as in April or Spring the opening of the year. Then the second Surah is Taurus or Baqarah, next is the Family of Imram which deals with the twins or Gemini. The twins in this instance would be Adam and Eve who according to the Quran were created the Remember and the second one a reference to Eve or even meaning two. There is a surah called the Bee which is Surah 16, this star cluster can be found in the Cancer constellation and is called Praesepe. Surah 10 Jonah is the star constellation Cetus or the Whale. Surah [113.1] speaks about Venus the morning star where it says: Say: I seek refuge in the Lord of the dawn. The Lord of the Dawn is the planet Venus which is the great morning star in the spring and the evening star in the autumn/fall. Surah 25:61 states "Blessed is He Who made the constellations in the heavens and made therein a lamp and a shining moon."

تَبَارَكَ الَّذِي جَعَلَ فِي السَّمَاءِ بُرُوجًا وَجَعَلَ فِيهَا سِرَاجًا وَقَمَرًا مُنِيرًا

Then we find in Surah 85:1 I swear by the mansions of the stars. The mansions of the stars relate to mansions in John 14:2 In my Father's house are many mansions: if it were not so, I would have told you. I go to prepare a place for you. You can also see where the writers of the Quran used symbolism with stars and the personification of the descendants of Abraham, for instance in Surah [12.4] "When Yusuf said to his father: O my father! surely, I saw eleven stars and the sun and the moon-- I saw them making obeisance to me."

إِذْ قَالَ يُوسُفُ لِأَبِيهِ يَا أَبَتِ إِنِّي رَأَيْتُ أَحَدَ عَشَرَ كَوْكَبًا وَالشَّمْسَ وَالْقَمَرَ رَأَيْتُهُمْ لِي سَاجِدِينَ

This speaking of the 13 tribes of Israel which includes the tribe of Dinah the only woman mentioned. The same is told in Islamic history. Dinah gives us Dinul Allah or the religion of Allah called Islam. There are 12 tribes of Ishmael and one daughter named Mahalath or Basemath and she represents the moon in Surah 12:4 "Now these are the generations of Ishmael, Abraham's son, whom Hagar the Egyptian, Sarah's handmaid, bore unto Abraham: And these are the names of the sons of Ishmael, by their names, according to their generations: The firstborn of Ishmael, Nebajoth, and Kedar, and Adbeel, and Mibsam, and Mishma, and Dumah, and Massa, Hadad and Tema, Jetur, Naphish and Kedmah.

These are the sons of Ishmael, and these are their names, by their towns and by their encampments; twelve princes according to their nations." Genesis 25:12-16

וְאֵלֶּה, שְׁמוֹת בְּנֵי יִשְׁמָעֵאל, בִּשְׁמֹתָם, לְתוֹלְדֹתָם: בְּכֹר יִשְׁמָעֵאל נְבָיֹת וְקֵדָר וְאַדְבְּאֵל וּמִבְשָׂם

וּמִשְׁמָע וְדוּמָה, וּמַשָּׂא

חֲדַד וְתֵימָא, יְטוּר נָפִישׁ וָקֵדְמָה

    Astronomy teaches us the sun moves 1 degree every 72 years on its 25,920 procession. The number 72 appears in numerous Islamic legends, namely the number of warriors on the Muslim side at the Battle of Badr. As well as the number of people martyred along with Imam Hussain at the Battle of Karbala. Other legends in Islam say 72 is the number of sects or denominations that are doomed to Hell, according to Hadith (Sayings of prophet Muhammad). "Islamic legend says the prophet Muhammad was in a cave for 3 days and 3 nights meditating." This relates to the astrological phenomena called the Winter solstice where the sun appears to stand still for 3 days and 3 nights every December 21 – 24 and 3 days 3 nights is 72 hours. The reader should understand this association with the Sun as Muslims pray based on the movement of the sun the same way the Jews in the bible prayed 3 times a day based on the movement of the Sun. 1 Samuel 20:[41] "And as soon as the lad was gone, David arose out of a place toward the south, and fell on his face to the ground, and bowed himself three times: and they kissed one another, and wept one with another, until David exceeded."

הַנַּעַר, בָּא, וְדָוִד קָם מֵאֵצֶל הַנֶּגֶב, וַיִּפֹּל לְאַפָּיו אַרְצָה וַיִּשְׁתַּחוּ שָׁלֹשׁ פְּעָמִים; וַיִּשְּׁקוּ אִישׁ אֶת-רֵעֵהוּ, וַיִּבְכּוּ אִישׁ אֶת-רֵעֵהוּ, עַד-דָּוִד, הִגְדִּיל

The similarities between the Jewish prophet David and Muhammad are interesting to say the least. As David was dying Bathsheba came to him, the name Bathsheba means daughter of the oath or seven. With his head resting on Aisha's lap, Muhammad asked her to dispose of his last worldly goods (seven coins). The reader can determine if this is a coincidence or if this was plagiarism by Arabs of the Jewish story of King David.

David	Muhammad
Looks upon Bathsheba's beauty (2 Samuels 6:7)	Looks upon Zaynab's beauty (Maulana Ali Quran)
Married Bathsheba (2 Samuels 11:26-27)	Married Zaynab (Yusef Ali Quran Surah 33:37)
Bathsheba's husband killed in Battle	Zaynab's husband Zayd killed in Battle
In his dying days was cared for by a Virgin named Abishag (1 Kings 1:2)	In his dying days was cared for by a Virgin named Aisha (Sayings of Muhammad, pg 7)
Had many wives	Had many wives
King of the Jews	Kings of the Arabs

ESSENTIAL OILS

The Prophet Muhammad (Peace and Blessings Be Upon Him) said, "There are three things of this world I have been made to prefer – prayer, wives and scents."

As a way to bring about calmness and a more spiritual vibe, essential oils have been used in various ancient cultures. Essential oils are oils that are made from plants like leaves, herbs, barks, and rinds. You can smell them, rub them on your skin, or put them in your bath. Essential oils like Camphor, Calamus, Cedarwood, Frankincense, Jasmine, Marjoram, Myrrh, Neroli, Rose, Sweet Basil and Thyme are mentioned in the Quran, Ahadith and other sacred Islamic texts. Surah Ar- Rahman, 12, 13: Therein are fruits, date-palms producing sheathed fruit-stalks (enclosing dates). And also corn, with (its) leaves and stalk for fodder, and sweet-scented plants

In Islam specifically, Rosewater is used by Muslims prior to salaat. Metaphysically, Rosewater elicits the emotion of love. Rosewater is a spiritually healing plant, it is good for the heart chakra. This again is another hidden reference to Venus, the Goddess or planet of love. Prior to making salaat, Muslims perform a ritual bathing called wuḍū' also called ablution, it is used in Islam as a form of purification and cleansing. Muslims wash their hands, face, and feet to ceremonially cleanse impurities before prayer or handling the Quran. These are strategic places of the body that allow maximum essential benefits. For example, essential oils placed on the bottom of the feet take approximately 20 minutes to travel to the amygdala and pineal gland in the brain. Most importantly, due to the properties of these oils, they do not disrupt the body's natural balance. Certain essential oils are used to stimulate various glands in the body to bring about a more spiritual environment. For example,, the Pineal gland is stimulated by fragrances such as Frankincense, Myrrh, Cedar wood, and Sandalwood. This accounts for the reason frankincense, myrrh and sandalwood are used in temples all over the world because it was known they affect mood.

The scent of an essential oil impacts the brain through the olfactory system because when a fragrance is inhaled, the odor molecules travel up the nose, and are trapped by olfactory membranes. These membranes contain approximately 800 million nerve endings, which receive the micro-fine, vaporized oil particles. They are carried along the axon of the nerve fibers and connected with the secondary neurons in the olfactory bulb in the brain. The olfactory bulb then transmits the impulses to the limbic system which is directly connected to areas of the brain that control heart rate, blood pressure, breathing, memory, stress levels and hormone balance.

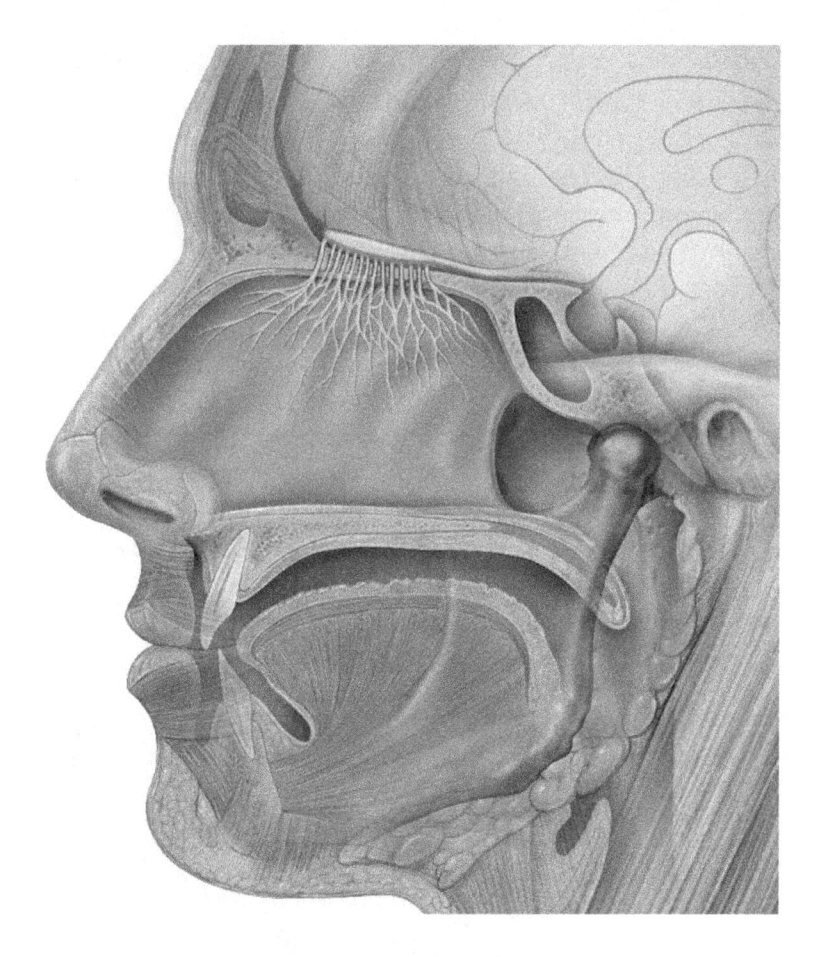

Olfactory System

In ancient Egypt, the use of Essential Oils now known as Aromatherapy was a way of balancing the auric field with the physical body. The sense of smell is depicted on the Egyptian walls by a woman smelling a lotus flower. The ancient Egyptians understood the olfactory bulbs stimulate the amygdala gland through smell and the science of Aromatherapy is one of the easiest ways to bring about a balance of the physical body with the auric fields. Further proof of the Ancient Egyptians use of essential oils was confirmed in King Tutankhamun's tomb, as it had alabaster jars that contained 350 liters of frankincense, myrrh and balsam oils. These oils were later used by other cultures in their religious ceremonies. According to the Old Testament, Israel's King Hezekiah kept 'the spices, and precious ointment' together with silver and gold in the royal treasure chamber (2 Kings, 20:13).

The New Testament also confirms the use of Essential oils. These three oils were also bought to Al Masih, the Christ, at his birth according Matthew chapter 2:11 "And when they were come into the house, they saw the young child with Mary his mother, and fell down, and worshipped him: and when they had opened their treasures, they presented unto him gifts; gold, and frankincense, and myrrh." Balsam was also referred to as gold according to the Hebrew University of Israel.

Three Wise Men

The ancients knew the heart is a hundred thousand times more electrical than the brain and five thousand times more magnetic. The heart chakra is green and associated with both love and the planet Venus. The heart is the center of the emotional body and emotions like solids have frequencies. The difference between the two is in the varying degrees of frequencies. Albert Einstein supposedly said, "Everything in Life is vibration."

In simpler terms at the physical level, frequency is the measurement of how quickly foundational cells are circulating and regenerating within the body. The greater the movement within the cells, the freer your body is to heal itself. This is experienced when one has a fever. When the body is in a state of dis-ease the cells vibrate at a higher frequency to force the removal of viruses via sweat or elimination of mucus, urine and/or feces. The slower the cells move within the body, the greater the chance for tumors, blockages, and diseases to develop. Thus, the use of essential oils helped the emotional body as well as the physical body because essential oils have frequencies. Therefore, when accompanied by positive thoughts the effectiveness of essentials oils increased exponentially.

Essential oils in the higher frequency ranges tend to influence the spirituality of the user. Essentials oils that vibrate on middle range frequencies tend to have an effect on the emotional body. Essential oils in the lower frequencies have more effect on structural and physical changes, including cells, hormones, and bones, as well as viruses, bacteria, and fungi. There have been experiments which measure the bio-frequency of essential oils. These studies show that essential oils accompanied by positive thoughts show on average and increase in the bio-frequency of those essential oils by 10 MHz Negative thoughts and words decreased frequency by 12 MHz on average. It was also identified that prayer increase the MHz of those essential oils by 15 MHz Thus, it lets us know the writers of the gospels of Mark and John knew about the healing powers of essential oils. Mark 6:13 And they cast out many devils, and anointed with oil many that were sick, and healed them. The book of John tells the story of how Nikodemus used oils to anoint the body of Al Masih, the Messiah. John 19:39 And there came also Nicodemus, which at the first came to Jesus by night, and brought a mixture of myrrh and aloes, about a hundred-pound weight. The Torah had many examples of essential oils. Here are a few more examples as found in the Old Testament. Author Dr. David Stewart, author of Healing Oils of the Bible. Gives us the following:

"Exodus 30:34-36 "And the Lord said unto Moses, Take unto thee sweet spices, stacte, and onycha, and galbanum; these sweet spices with pure frankincense: of each there shall be a like weight".

Ancient Uses: Holy anointing oil, various medicines, perfume, spiritually uplifting yet grounding, pain relief, spasms and cramps, diuretic.

Modern Uses: Abscesses, acne, asthma, chronic coughs, cramps, indigestion, muscular aches and pains, scar tissue, wrinkles, wounds, emotionally balancing.

This oil allows for the shedding of old ideas and outdated behavior and attitudes, resulting in total surrender to the Creator. It sheds light on life's purpose and on the inner self. This oil may unveil sadness, wrongdoing, untruthfulness and crimes against the soul. It communicates with the deeper layers of self, allowing for gradual unfolding of truth. It is used to balance extreme or intense emotions. This oil is the main ingredient in the blend

"Gathering" because it aligns the brain with a person's spiritual purpose.

1 Kings 4:33
Cedar wood "And he spake of trees, from the cedar tree that is in Lebanon even unto the hyssop that springeth out of the wall"..

    The cedars of Lebanon were used to build Solomon's Temple and Herod's Temple. Cedar was an integral part of two biblical purification rituals; one was used for lepers and another for those who were impure from touching a dead body (Leviticus 14:1-32; Numbers 19). The ritual for cleansing leprosy used cedar wood and hyssop oils. They were applied to the tip or top of the right ear, the right thumb, and the right toe. In reflexology and emotional release, that portion of the ear is where one releases and resolves issues regarding their parents. The thumb and big toe are the trigger points for clearing fears of the unknown and mental blocks against learning. The big toe is a point for clearing addictions and compulsive behavior. The scent of cedar wood can help clear many buried emotions, including feelings of pride or conceit.

    Cedar wood was used by the Egyptians and Sumerians for embalming, for ritual purposes, as a disinfectant and for other medicinal purposes. It is still actively used in Tibetan medicine and as a meditation aid by Tibetan Buddhists and others. It is thought to enhance spirituality and strengthen our connection with the Divine. Native American Indians used "Cedar" in purification. Inhaling Cedar wood oil relaxes an over-analytical mind. Use Cedar wood oil before and after business meetings to generate greater clarity, to quickly perceive the core issue or to get to the point. Cedar wood has a purifying energy that helps to release emotional toxins. This oil is most effective with ADD children. Lastly, a few other uses are hair loss, tuberculosis, bronchitis, gonorrhea and skin disorders.

    Modern science now shows us that frankincense has the ability to increase the oxygen around the pineal and pituitary gland, therefore stimulating the pineal gland through which we communicate spiritually. Practically speaking it has a centering effect on the emotions. It can slow respiration, thus helping your body calm and center itself. Frankincense has a delightfully sweet and slightly spicy odor. It can act as an expectorant, soothing congestion. It is a wonderful oil to blend into facial creams or oils to reverse aging skin. The ancients used it as well for embalming. Modern uses supports healing cancer, depression, allergies, headaches, bronchitis, herpes, tonsillitis, typhoid, warts, brain damage, stimulates body's production of white corpuscles (immune builder), expectorant. Can help with memory. Opens the 3rd Eye for connection. Note that the Hebrew word for frankincense, lebonah (sometimes translated as "incense"), is in the Bible 22 times.

Exodus 12:22

Hyssop- (Hyssopus officinalis)

Caution for those with High Blood Pressure or Epilepsy should not use the following oil -

The hyssop plant was used during the exodus from Egypt to dab the Hebrews' doorposts with lamb's blood, protecting them from the plague of death.

ALLAH, THE QURAN, VENUS AND YOU

Psalms 51:7 (Used for spiritual purification)
"Purge me with hyssop, and I shall be clean: wash me, and I shall be whiter than snow".

Ancient Uses: Drove away evil spirits. Also spiritually uplifting, meditation, spiritual purification, various medicines, respiratory relief, decongestant, expectorant.

Jesus was offered Hyssop on the cross. Why? Crucifixion is death by slow suffocation as one's lungs gradually fill up with fluid and you can't breathe nor have the strength to lift yourself, nor cough. Hyssop may have been offered as an act of mercy to those dying by crucifixion to help ease their congestion and give them some relief both physically and emotionally. Rubbing Hyssop oil on the shoulders helps reduce the tension from carrying emotional burdens. Using Hyssop on the lung reflex points of the hands and feet helps break up congestion produced by inwardly grieving. Massaging with deep pressure into the colon reflex points of the hands and feet helps release stagnated energy from the colon and purges toxins from the physical body. Hyssop belongs to the mint family. It is a strong oil and can be irritating to some people's skin, but is safe in the palms and safe to inhale for everyone.

Modern Uses: Promotes permanent healing at a cellular level. Helps to relieve anxiety, arthritis, asthma, respiratory infections, parasites, sore throats, cuts and wounds. Metabolizes fat, increases perspiration, detoxifying, and emotional balancing.

Myrrh- (commiphora myrrha)

Myrrh is a gum resin from a shrubby tree, which grows in Yemen and neighboring regions of Africa. The fruit is smooth and somewhat larger than a pea. The color of myrrh varies from pale reddish-yellow to reddish-brown or red. Myrrh and Frankincense both are resins that come from trees that have to be 100 years old before you can tap the resins. Myrrh contains many compounds that are individually toxic, yet in combination, they make up an oil that is one of the safest, mildest, gentlest oils in nature.

Ancient Uses: Pregnant mothers anointed themselves for protection against infectious diseases and to elevate feelings of well-being. It was used during labor to massage on perineum to facilitate stretching. Used after childbirth to prevent or remove abdominal stretch marks. Customarily used on umbilical cords of newborn to protect the naval from infection.

Myrrh is anti-infectious and supports the immune system. The Arabian people find it beneficial for skin conditions; such as athletes foot, chapped and cracked skin, eczema, insect repellent, oral hygiene, ringworm, wounds and wrinkles. It is used to help with asthma, bronchitis, catarrh, coughs, gingivitis, mouth ulcers and sore throat. It may also help alleviate diarrhea, dyspepsia, flatulence, fungal infection, and hemorrhoids. It can decongest the prostrate and normalizes hyper-thyroid problems. The ancients embalmed their dead with myrrh, because of its antibacterial qualities.

For thousands of years, even to the present day, myrrh has been used by perfumers to blend with more volatile oils to make their fragrances last longer. Virtually all of the therapeutic ointments mentioned throughout the

Bible contained myrrh so that the oils blended in the ointment would exert their healing properties for longer periods of time in the body. It was used so universally in Biblical ointments that the Greek word for ointment (muron) is also the Greek word for myrrh. Egyptians carried cones of fat on their heads containing Myrrh that would melt in the desert heat and keep their bodies bathed in Myrrh probably to keep insects away, but also, and the oil also works as a sunshield, protecting our skin from sun damage. Egyptians used it for that purpose for thousands of years. Myrrh contains high amounts of sesquiterpenes, compounds that have direct effects on the hypothalamus, pituitary, and amygdala, the seat of our emotions. Those who have experienced myrrh know of its great calming effect. It is good for people who are afraid to speak up about their emotions. The oil creates confidence and awareness. It moves fluids and so it is good for weight loss. Its centering properties make it an excellent inhalation for compulsive eaters, in part because it connects them with the real issues and does not allow them to hide behind their food.

Myrtle- (Myrtus communis)
To the ancient Jews, myrtle was symbolic of peace and justice. One of the promises to Israel for the future is that "instead of the brier shall come up the myrtle tree" (Isaiah 55:13). Myrtle has been studied for its soothing effects on the respiratory system. This oil is helpful with allergies because it helps us gain insight into the something or someone that we are irritated with. Myrtle has been researched by Dr. Penoel, a French expert on essential oils, for normalizing hormonal imbalances of the thyroid and ovaries. It balances hypothyroidism. It is also a liver stimulant and may release anger.

ALLAH, THE QURAN, VENUS AND YOU

Onycha- (Styrax benzoin)
Exodus 30:34
"And the Lord said unto Moses, Take unto thee sweet spices, stacte, and onycha, and galbanum; these sweet spices with pure frankincense: of each shall there be a like weight." Like frankincense and myrrh, onycha is a resin. It was traditionally known for its comforting and soothing properties. It is the heaviest oil of all and also smells like vanilla. Onycha valued lies in its ability to speed the healing of wounds and prevent infection.

Rose of Sharon/Cistus- (Labdanum-Cisius ladanifer):
Song of Solomon 2:1
"I am the Rose of Sharon, and the lily of the valley" It is thought that the Cistus oil comes from a plant rock rose. It is beautiful rose which has a soft honey-like scent and may be the small shrubby tree called the Rose of Sharon. Anciently, the gum that exudes from this plant was collected from the hair of goats that had browsed among the bushes. This is a fragrance of prophecy, visions and all quests for truth. This oil remains useful and excellent for auto-immune system. The oil should be used along the spine. Cistus has also been studied for its effects on cell regeneration.

Spikenard- (Nardostachys jatamansi)
Mark 14:3
"And Jesus being in Bethany, in the house of Simon the leper, as he sat at meat, there came a woman having an alabaster box of ointment of spikenard, very precious, and she brake the box, and poured the ointment on his head.

When a distinguished guest came visiting, the master of the house showed honor by breaking open the spikenard and anointing the guest. The Hebrews and the Romans used spikenard in the burial of their dead. This is why Jesus said of the woman who poured the precious spikenard oil on Him, "She is come a forehand to anoint my body to the burying" (Mark 14:8). Spikenard helps to soothe and nourish the skin. It is one of the best oils for calming the nerves. It is grounding and settles an out-of-balance mind. It is a post-digestive oil in India. (One drop taken near the end of the meal calms the stomach.) It is a stimulant to the male hormonal system. It brings courage and power. It helps people feel in charge of their lives. In preparation for the departure of the spirit to the heavens, Spikenard allows us to release our fears of the unknown and have the courage to step forward. Spikenard helps to reconcile all that has happened to us in this lifetime upon the earth, and to make peace with those who have hurt us. It is the fragrance of forgiveness. Spikenard was transported to the Holy Land in sealed alabaster boxes all the way from the Himalayan Mountains. Stewart, David, Healing *Oils of the Bible.* (2003)

The use of essential oil was and its properties was discovered much later by Europeans. Research at Eastern State University discovered the following;

In 1992, it was discovered that pure essential oils have a bioelectrical frequency. Bruce Tainio, of Tainio Technology (an independent division of Eastern State University) in Cheny, Washington, created a bio-frequency monitor to calculate this frequency. He found the average frequency of a human body is between 62-68 Hz. Dr. Robert O'Becker (The Body Electric) states "much about a person's health can be determined by the frequency of the person's body." If the frequency drops, the immune system is compromised. Colds and flu symptoms appear at 58 Hz, Candida at 55 Hz, Epstein Barr virus at 52 Hz and Cancer at 42 Hz.

Dr. Gary Young noticed in his private practice, that when using essential oils patients begin to feel emotionally rejuvenated at first and then within seconds their symptoms start to abate and pain decreased 50 - 80% within 3 minutes. This led him to doing work with Bruce Tainio on oil frequency measurements.

Recent research in Japan has confirmed that synthetic floral perfumes can limit brain function while pure essential oils enhance the range and activity of brain function within twenty seconds of inhalation. One study found the test scores and alertness of students increased by 28% when pure peppermint oil was diffused in the classroom of students while learning and later during the testing periods. To substantiate this claim of increased brain function, another study conducted by Japanese researchers found that inhaling lemon oil helps cut rates of error by computer operators by up to 50%. The world news recently reported a Japanese study stating that a chemical that stimulates the burning of body fat is released after inhaling a mixture of essential oils containing grapefruit, black pepper, tarragon, and fennel.

Dr. Jean Valnet an M.D. from France, who is a medical researcher and essential oil expert, says about clove oil, "it has been found to have electronic constituents which are opposed to cancer and viral diseases." So we can see the high frequency of the oils can raise the electrical frequency of our body, creating an environment in which low frequency organisms cannot function.
http://www.heavenlyscent.net/frequency.htm taken 3/6/17

Note, it is extremely imperative that the reader learns about the frequencies/vibration of foods that are ingested. Male or non-electric foods have a low frequency, whereas female and electric foods have a very high frequency.

- Processed / canned food had zero MHz frequency

- Fresh produce measured up to 15 MHz frequency

- Dried herbs measured from 12- 22 MHz

- Fresh herbs measured from 20-27 MHZ

- Essential oils measured from 52 MHz – 320 MHz

Essential oils at a minimum should contain a proper balance of constituents. They must be pure (organic) with no artificial substances to block the system and should be of the proper frequency. Since the astral and physical bodies vibrate in order to maintain a healthy environment for the body it should maintain a frequency of 60 megahertz. The following is a list of essential oils and the types of dis-ease they aid in curing.

Frequencies of Single Essential Oils and Blends

SINGLE ESSENTIAL OILS					
Angelica	85 MHz	Christmas Spirit	104 MHz	Magnify Your Purpose	99 MHz
Basil	52 MHz	Citrus Fresh	90 MHz	Melrose	48 MHz
Frankincense	147 MHz	Clarity	101 MHz	Mister	147 MHz
Galbanum	56 MHz	Di-Tone	102 MHz	Motivation	103 MHz
German Chamomile	105 MHz	Dragon Time	72 MHz	M-Grain	72 MHz
Helichrysum	181 MHz	Dream Catcher	98 MHz	PanAway	112 MHz
Idaho Tansy	105 MHz	EndoFlex	138 MHz	Peace & Calming	105 MHz
Juniper	98 MHz	En-R-Gee	106 MHz	Present Time	98 MHz
Lavender	118 MHz	Envision	90 MHz	Purification	46 MHz
Melissa (lemon balm)	102 MHz	Exodus II	180 MHz	Raven	70 MHz
Myrrh	105 MHz	Forgiveness	192 MHz	R.C.	75 MHz
Peppermint	78 MHz	Gathering	99 MHz	Release	102 MHz
Ravintsara	134 MHz	Gentle Baby	152 MHz	Relieve It	56 MHz
Rose	320 MHz	Grounding	140 MHz	Sacred Mountain	176 MHz
Sandalwood	96 MHz	Harmony	101 MHz	SARA	102 MHz
		Hope	98 MHz	Sensation	88 MHz
		Humility	88 MHz	Surrender	98 MHz
ESSENTIAL OIL BLENDS		ImmuPower	89 MHz	Thieves	150 MHz
Abundance	78 MHz	Inner Child	98 MHz	3 Wise Men	72 MHz
Acceptance	102 MHz	Inspiration	141 MHz	Trauma Life	92 MHz
Aroma Life	84 MHz	Into the Future	88 MHz	Valor	47 MHz
Aroma Siez	64 MHz	Joy	188 MHz	White Angelica	89 MHz
Awaken	89 MHz	Juva Flex	82 MHz		
Brain Power	78 MHz	Live With Passion	89 MHz		

Essential Oils Chart

Here are other essentials oils and the ailments they report to remedy. As with all remedies, it is advised that the reader consult with a medical professional before applying and employing the use of essential oils.

Basil - digestion, insomnia, anxiety, mental fatigue, asthma

Benzoin - oily skin, fluid retention, muscle pain, asthma, wounds

Bergamot - digestion, acne, eczema, depression, anxiety, oily skin, vaginitis, cystitis, asthma, wounds

Camomile - digestion, insomnia, menstrual pain, eczema, depression, anxiety, dry skin, fluid retention, pms, allergies, muscle pain, stress, asthma, wounds

Cypress – aids in the alleviation of several ailments and transitional periods

Cypress oil is helpful in times of transition such as career changes, moving homes, menopause and major spiritual decisions. Cypress also helps with painful transitions such as bereavement or the ending of close relationships. It helps re-establish the ability to flow with life without the anxiety of deciding what the next step is or how it will unfold. It offers strength and energetic protection to those who are vulnerable and insecure or have lost their purpose. It can be used to move on from a situation. Using Cypress oil on the spleen point under the left rib cage clears blockages in energy flow and supports better assimilation of food. Cypress is used to support the circulatory system. Cypress is good for anything in excess. It is very grounding. It is a balancer of the female system and is often combined with clary sage for hot flashes and is used to reduce or inhibit ovarian cysts. It also helps to build

ALLAH, THE QURAN, VENUS AND YOU

the immune system, controls hemorrhages and nose bleeds, increases circulation, strengthens blood capillaries, and aids in relieving angina pains. Also good for arthritis, laryngitis, reducing scar tissue and menstrual cramps.

Eucalyptus - digestion, stomach, fluid retention, sprains, cystitis, allergies, muscle pain, asthma, wounds

Frankincense - digestion, eczema, oily skin, cystitis, asthma, wounds

Geranium - acne, fungi, eczema, depression, anxiety, dry skin, fluid retention, varicose veins, sprains, pms, stress

Juniper - digestion, acne, dandruff, cellulite, insomnia, menstrual pain, eczema, anxiety, mental fatigue, oily skin, fluid retention, varicose veins, cystitis, muscle pain, wounds

Lavender – Lavender essential oil also displays promising results in treating hair loss, in particular with patients suffering from *alopecia*, an autoimmune condition where the hair follicles are rejected by the body. In Scotland, a study showed that 40% of *alopecia* test subjects reported an increase in hair growth after regularly rubbing lavender essential oil on their scalp.

Lemon - dandruff, stomach, oily skin, varicose veins, asthma

Mandarin – colds

Marjoram - headaches, digestion, insomnia, menstrual pain, colds, mental fatigue, sprains, muscle pain, stress, asthma

Myrrh - digestion, stomach, pms, wounds

ALLAH, THE QURAN, VENUS AND YOU

Neroli - insomnia, menstrual pain, stomach, depression, anxiety, dry skin, oily skin, muscle pain, stress, wounds

Patchouli - cellulite, stress, depression, dry skin

Peppermint - headaches, digestion, menstrual pain, colds, anxiety, varicose veins, acne,

Rose - headaches, cellulite, insomnia, colds, depression, sprains, cystitis, muscle pain, stress, wounds

Rosemary - headaches, digestion, dandruff, cellulite, stomach, anxiety, oily skin, fluid retention, sprains, allergies, asthma, wounds

Sandalwood - pretty much everything although not quite as powerful as lavender

Tea Tree Oil - fungi of all sorts, stomach

Ylang Ylang - insomnia, menstrual pain, stomach, depression, anxiety, dry skin, oily skin, muscle pain, stress, wounds

Lord of Sirius

In Africa one of the most ancient Gods was Asar misnomer Osiris. Osiris was the husband and consort of Aset misnomer Isis known in the Quran as Al Uzza. Isis was also associated with the Egyptian deity Sopdet. Sopdet was her ancient Egyptian name and she was associated with the star Sirius called by the Greeks Sothis. Thus, one has to wonder how did the word Sirius end up in the Quran as we find in Surah 53 called An Najm (the Star) [53.49] And that He is the Lord of the Sirius; Sirius is the brightest star in the Northern Hemisphere skies. It was adorned by the Egyptians because every year on its helical rising the Hapi misnomer Nile river would flood, thus it became very important.

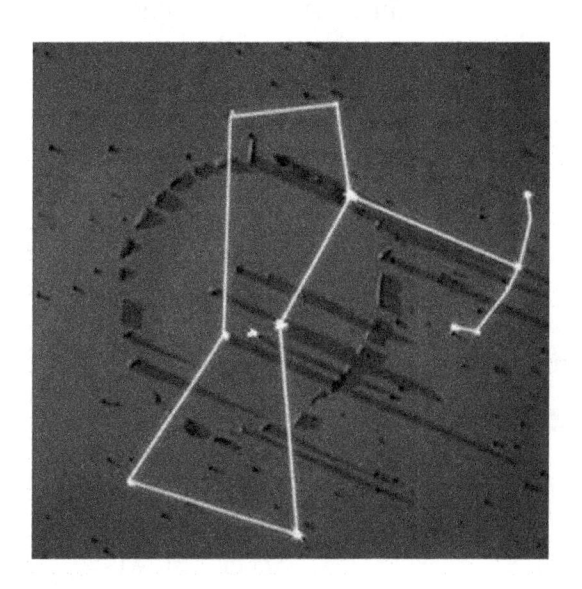

Sirius was called the star in the East in biblical times and is the star the wise men followed to look for the baby Jesus called by Muslims, Isa (pronounced Ee-sa). As we learned in God, The Bible, The Planets and Your Body this is allegory for the star constellation called Sah by the Egyptians misnomer Orion by Greeks, Romans and other

Europeans. Sah later became associated with the Egyptian deity Osiris. As Egyptian cosmology begin to take form in Nabta Playa it later reached its apex in Southern Egypt now known as Cairo. Nabta Playa is found in the Nubian desert and is about 500 miles north of Cairo and about 62 miles south of Abu Simbel. In Nabta Playa there sits a megalith of stones that predate Stonehenge and is aligned to the star constellation Sah (Orion). This star calendar was used by the ancient Africans as far back as 12,000 years ago and helped form the basis for their complex cosmology.

    This cosmology was later reproduced in later subsequent cultures and fraternities. A more notable fraternity that used this concept was that of the infamous Skull and Bones. As you recognize the constellation Sah also known as Orion is missing his head (skull) and legs (bones). Sah is a seven-star constellation with 3 stars in its belt and 2 stars in the shoulder area and 2 stars in the thigh area (322) This is the mystery behind Skull and Bones whose symbol is an owl because in the word knowledge is hidden the word OWL. According to the book Animal Speaks; "Owls represent silent or higher wisdom, prophecy, mystery, healing power, hidden secrets, seeing in the darkness, spiritual sight, death, smelting, thunderbolt, purification, communion and a symbol of spirit or ghost leading from death to life. The hooting of the great horned owl is thought to be a harbinger of spring". (Andrew, Ted, Dictionary of Symbols, Chevalier & Gheerbrant; Animal Speak, Llewellyn

Worldwide, LTD. (2002. Knowledge is found in the skull. Later cut off their head and legs at burial. This includes the story of John the Baptist whose head was decapitated at the request of Salome the daughter of Herodotus.

Star Constellations

Sah (Orion), Narmer, Ba'al

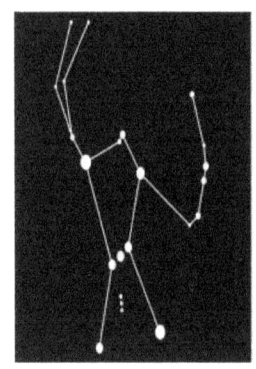

Sah/Orion

Star constellations were anthropomorphic and were considered masculine if their helical rising was before the sun, however when a star constellation followed the sun it was considered feminine. The constellation Sah became Asar (Orion) and was then made into the story of Narmer/Menes who was the first pharaoh of the dynastic periods according to European Egyptologists. However, the Palermo stone indicates there were more pharaohs that predate Narmer/Menes. The Narmer palette shows him in the smiting pose just as the star constellation Sah. It was later used by the Sumerians, Babylonians, Canaanites as their deity Ba'al meaning Lord, just as he is called in Surah 53:49 of the Quran, where it states in Arabic Rabu Ashurah – Lord of Sirius. وَأَنَّهُ هُوَ رَبُّ الشِّعْرَىٰ

This hijacking of the stories was also used with the star constellation Virgo, which became Aset and her son Heru (Horus) and later Jesus and his mother Mary. There leaves little room for conjecture at this point it is so obvious how these stories came into existence.

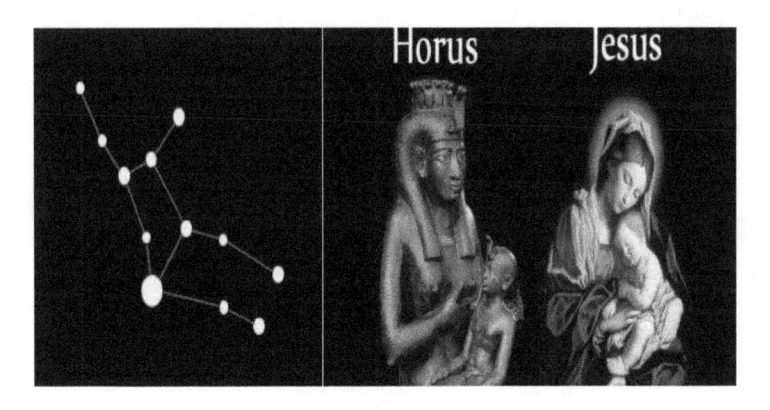

Virgo/Aset

As these ancient people refined their cosmologies, they began to create temples and more elaborate stories of their deities called by them Neteru. The story of Abraham (Ibrahim) and his wife Sarah was recreated from the Osiris/Isis cosmology. Where Osiris married his sister the same way Abram (Abraham) called Sarai (Sarah) his wife and sister in the bible. Ba'al is a word that means husband and the feminine aspect of Ba'al is Ba'alah meaning Princess or Lady of the House. The same way Sarai means Princess.

These ancient Africans were acknowledgers of both feminine and masculine aspects of the divine. Which is why the concept of as above so below is ever so present in ancient African architecture. Not only did they study the stars and make elaborate cosmologies about them by personifying them into human deities. They took it a step further by designing their temples in the form of the female body of the deity Aset, Sopdet, Isis aka Sirius. There is a temple in Philae, Egypt dedicated to the deity Isis. The hieroglyph for Isis is that of a woman and a throne. Looking at the temple of Isis in Philae you see a replica of the throne.

Temple of Aset in Philae

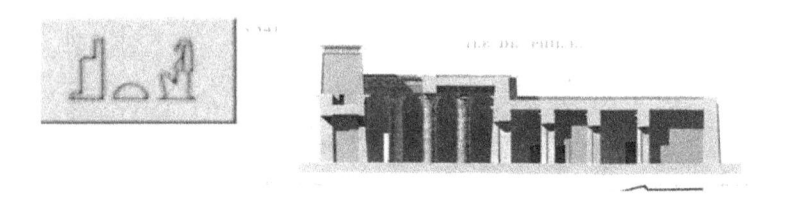

Temple of Aset

     She is sometimes depicted sitting on her throne holding an ankh, the symbol for the key of life. Aset's name acutally means Throne and is really representative of the portion of our skull called physiologically the sphenoid bone, the pituitary gland sits inside this bone. Medically this is called in the latin language sella turcica. Sella meaning Seat or Throne and turcicia meaning Turkey. The pituitary gland controls the endocrine glands in the body. The endocrine glands are overlayed by the chakras which are energy wheels. The sphenoid bone sits in the front of the skull behind the sinuses and is attached to two greater wings on the lateral side of the body and two lesser wings from the anterior side.

There are hieroglyphs of Isis with the throne on her head with wings. This is representative of the sphenoid bone that is comprised of the middle section the sella turcica and the greater and lesser wings. Egyptians routinely meshed the various portions of the brain with their deities. Another example would be the Sun god Khepera who is the scarab deity whose hieroglyph resembles the cranium with sutures. Continually, the spine which is 18 inches long is the same length as a royal Egyptian cubit. The spine is at times represented as the zjed pillar routinely associated with Osiris. This shows the complexity of Egyptian cosmology, as it wasn't just an association between the stars, the Gods and the temples, it went even further to include aspects of the skeletal and endocrine systems. Striking a very delicate balance between that which is above and that which is below.

Aset

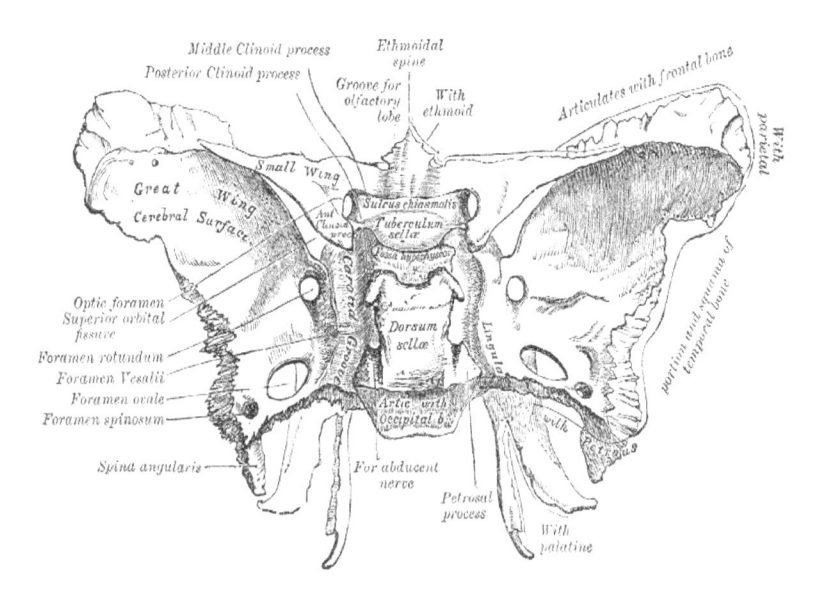

Sphenoid Bone

This is showing that they are identical. The Atom and the Even (Adam and Eve). Which again was taken from the cosmology of the Africans of the constellations Orion and Sirius. Orion comes from Or an Ion, an Ion is an atom or group of atoms that carries a positive or negative electric charge as a result of having lost or gained one or more electrons. The biblical creation story says that Allah (God) removed a rib from Adam and created Eve. The rib is found in the word for deoxyribonucleic acid (DNA). The bible is teaching you about splitting atoms. For an ion to exist an electron must be removed from an atom and when this happens it multiplies. The same way the rib was removed from Adam and created Eve aka the second one (untha in Arabic). وَمَا خَلَقَ الذَّكَرَ وَالْأُنْثَىٰ Surah 92:3 And He created you the male and the female. Eve became the isotope or Isis type to Adam or the Atom, which comes from the Egyptian deity Atum.

Isotope or Isis type. According to dictionary.com an Isotope is defined as the any of two or more forms of a chemical element, having the same number of protons in the nucleus, or the same atomic number, but having different numbers of neutrons in the nucleus, or different atomic weights. There are 275 isotopes of the 81 stable elements, in addition to over 800 radioactive isotopes, and every element has known isotopic forms. Isotopes of a single element possess almost identical properties. An Isotope 1913, literally "having the same place," from Greek isos "equal" (see iso-) + topos "place" (see topos); so called because, despite having different atomic weights, the various forms of an element occupy the same place on the periodic table.
https://www.etymonline.com/word/isotope#etymonline_v_12274 .

Therefore, the reader should begin to see a lot of the medical and scientific terminology that exist today comes from Egyptian cosmology and mysticism. Osiris represents the third eye, yet when viewed with the medical background one can reason out, Os a medical term meaning opening and Iris a part of the that determines the color of the eye. Thus, the Greek word Osiris is dealing with the fact Osiris is the third eye. If one continues to dissect the brain, images of these creator gods illuminate like the full moon on a super moon celestial event.

If you were to look at the brain from the ventral or underneath view, you would see portions of the Optic nerve, pyramid, pons, brain stem and other arteries that shows the body of a woman sitting on a throne, like Isis. This area of the brain is near the cerebellum and is also near a section of the brain called the uncus. The word uncus is medical term that comes from the Latin word uncus which means hook. Therefore, it should come as no surprise Isis is always shown carrying an ankh. European scholars who have not figured out the language of the Africans pass misinformation on to the world. They have told us the ankh means life. This is partially true. ANKH is an abbreviation for the word Aniko Heh meaning Life.

Ankh is Anchor which is a hook. If you look at an anchor it is shaped like an ankh. Thus, the words Ankh and Uncus sound the same phonetically. As you can see these things cannot be a coincidence. For we know the description of the 12 cranial nerves are found in Numbers 17:2 " take every one of them a rod according to the house of their father, to the house of their fathers, twelve rods."

אֱמֹר אֶל-אֶלְעָזָר בֶּן-אַהֲרֹן הַכֹּהֵן, וְיָרֵם אֶת-הַמַּחְתֹּת מִבֵּין הַשְּׂרֵפָה, וְאֶת-הָאֵשׁ, זְרֵה-הָלְאָה: כִּי, קָדֵשׁוּ

Then there is description of the sphenoid bone called the mercy seat in Exodus 25:20 "And the cherubims shall stretch forth their wings on high, covering the mercy seat with their wings."

וְהָיוּ הַכְּרֻבִים פֹּרְשֵׂי כְנָפַיִם לְמַעְלָה, סֹכְכִים בְּכַנְפֵיהֶם עַל-הַכַּפֹּרֶת, וּפְנֵיהֶם, אִישׁ אֶל-אָחִיו; אֶל-הַכַּפֹּרֶת--יִהְיוּ, פְּנֵי הַכְּרֻבִים.

This tells you the bible as well as the Quran are books on the physiology of the human body. Earlier in Surah al Baqara was the ayyat about the Throne "Allah! There is no god but He - the Living, The Self-subsisting, Eternal. No slumber can seize Him Nor Sleep. His are all things In the heavens and on earth. Who is there can intercede In His presence except As he permitteth? He knoweth What (appeareth to His creatures As) Before or After or Behind them. Nor shall they encompass Aught of his knowledge Except as He willeth. His throne doth extend Over the heavens And on earth, and He feeleth No fatigue in guarding And preserving them, For He is the Most High. The Supreme (in glory)."
[Surah al-Baqarah 2: 255]

اللَّهُ لَا إِلَٰهَ إِلَّا هُوَ الْحَيُّ الْقَيُّومُ ۚ لَا تَأْخُذُهُ سِنَةٌ وَلَا نَوْمٌ ۚ لَهُ مَا فِي السَّمَاوَاتِ وَمَا فِي الْأَرْضِ ۗ مَن ذَا الَّذِي يَشْفَعُ عِندَهُ إِلَّا بِإِذْنِهِ ۚ يَعْلَمُ مَا بَيْنَ أَيْدِيهِمْ وَمَا خَلْفَهُمْ ۖ وَلَا يُحِيطُونَ بِشَيْءٍ مِّنْ عِلْمِهِ إِلَّا بِمَا شَاءَ ۚ وَسِعَ كُرْسِيُّهُ السَّمَاوَاتِ وَالْأَرْضَ ۖ وَلَا يَئُودُهُ حِفْظُهُمَا ۚ وَهُوَ الْعَلِيُّ الْعَظِيمُ

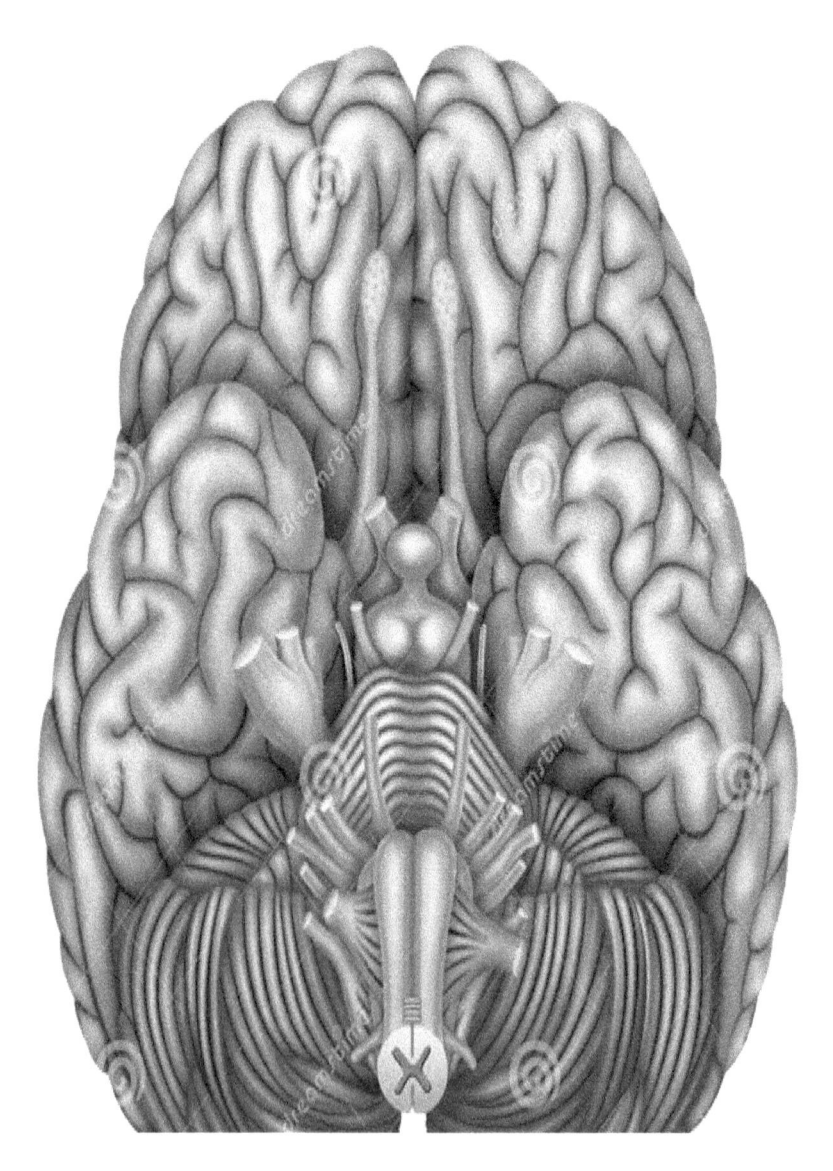

Ventral View of the Brain

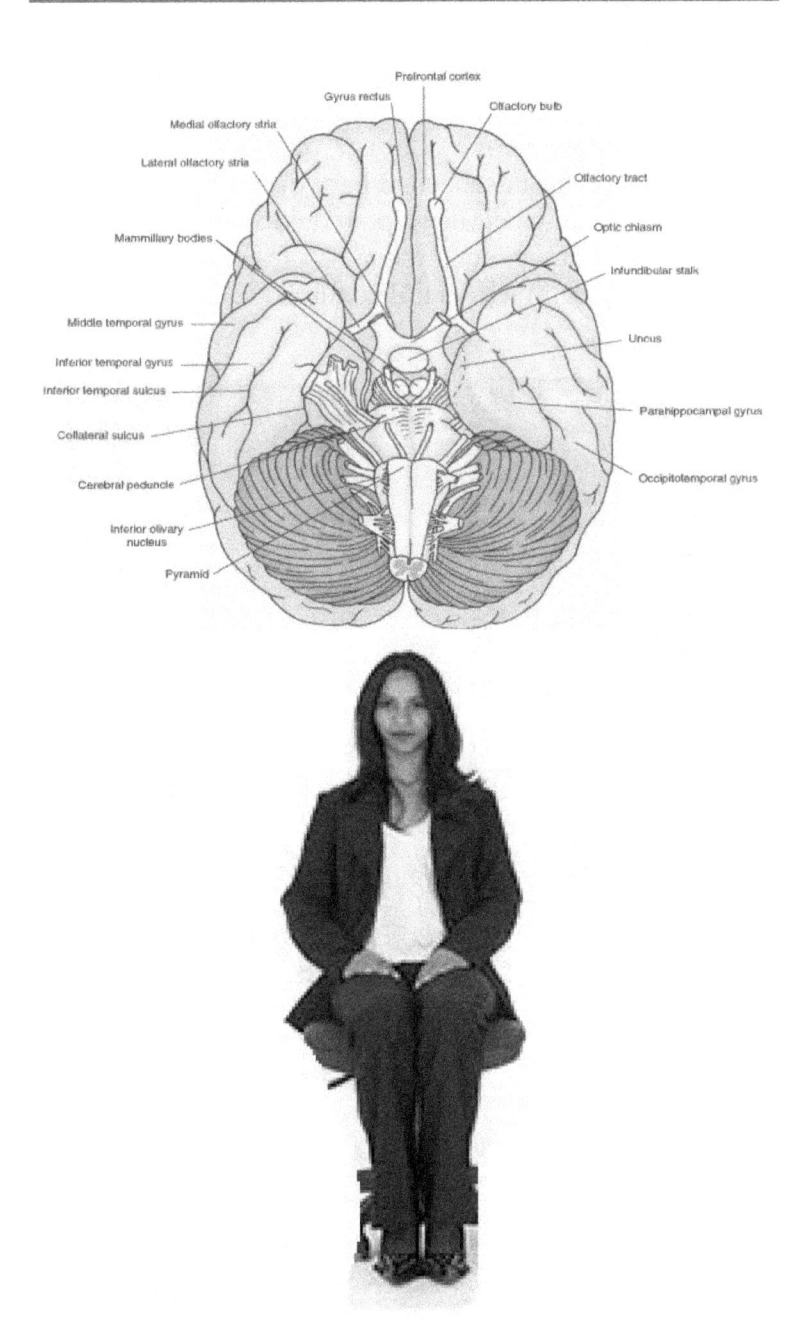

ALLAH, THE QURAN, VENUS AND YOU

Ventral View of Brain/Olfactory Bulb

121

Interestingly, as we view this section of the brain, we also see the olfactory bulb and olfactory tract making the Atef headdress worn by Osiris. Could it be the ancient Egyptians were this advanced to have dissected the brain and then associated their concept of deities as being associated with higher consciousness? The images and temples left by them leaves little doubt!

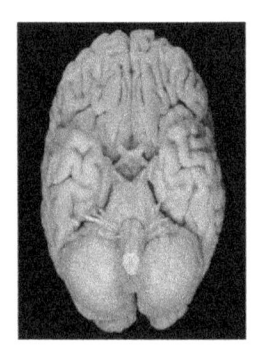

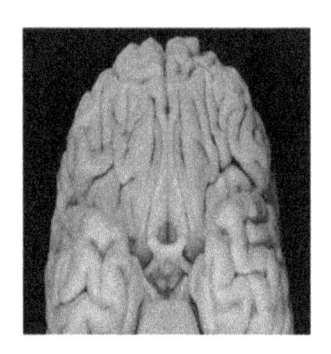

Atef Crown/Brain

Considering the first recorded genius was Imhotep who was ultimately defied as the god of architecture, medicine and science. He is the designer of the step pyramid in Saqqara for the Pharaoh Djoser/Zoser of the 3rd dynastic period. As a physician, he was practicing medicine over 2,000 years before the alleged father of medicine, Hippocrates. There exists a document known as the Edwin Smith Papyrus which has over 100 anatomical words, in addition, it lists almost 50 injuries along with their treatment and it believed to be a copy of Imhotep's earlier work. Multi-genius Imhotep was performing all types of surgeries. The Edwin Smith Papyrus contains knowledge of the cranial structure, external surface of the brain as well as the cerebral spinal fluid (CSF) called Chrism in Greek which bathes the brain and travels down the spinal cord.

Imhotep's knowledge of the human converted over to his architectural endeavors. The unit of measurement in Egypt was the Egyptian royal cubit called mh nswt and was from the tip of the middle finger to the bottom of the elbow. This usually measures to roughly 18 inches or about the same length as the spinal column. This again shows a direct correlation between the way Imhotep built religious structures and the human body as the Edwin Smith Papyrus speaks about paralysis and shows how to treat it. Recognizing when paralysis happened in the body a certain portion of the central nervous system inclusive of the spine was known.

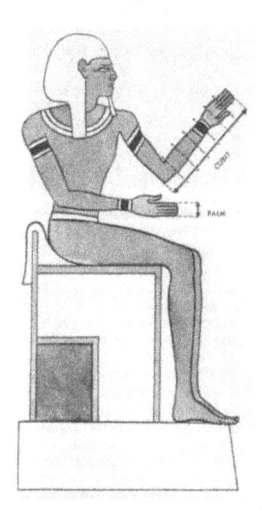

One of the most famous temples ever built in Egypt is the temple of Ipet-Isut misnomer Karnak. Ipet-Isut means "The Most Select (or Sacred) of Places. It is constructed like the human body and had hundreds of rams headed sphinx that lined up in the courtyard of the largest temple in the world. This temple became the basis of all religious structures as it is oriented to receive the rising sun in the east. The same way the human body receives the sun in the east when one wakes every morning. Ancient temples always had the temple oriented to east because the head of the human body is in the east. The head represents the holy of holies thus inside each temple was an area at the rear of that temple that contained an altar. On certain days of the year mainly the winter solstice the sun would rise and send a beam of light at the back of the temple and shine on the deity sitting on the altar. As you enter the temples in Egypt, you will notice the ceilings get lower the further you go into the temple. The floors elevate which gives the appearance of the temple capturing the suns light so that it shines on the third eye of the deity on the altar on those select days.

Secularly, we view the human body as the head being north, the feet south, the left hand west and the right hand east. However, this is not how it should be viewed esoterically. The head is the east side of the body, the feet in the west, the left hand is north and the right hand is south and accounts for why left-handed people are called south paws. This is why the temples in the ancient world are oriented to the east. In Islam the mihrabs in America are in the east inside the mosque/masjid. The word mihrab means the special place in the house which really denotes the holy of holies because it points to the east or the direction of prayer called Qiblah in Arabic. The mihrab is shaped like an arch inside of the mosque and represents the ancient symbol for women. Coincidently, there is a portion of the brain called the fornix which is Latin for arch. The fornix is connected to the Ammon's horn aka the hippocampus.

As you travel through Egypt you see other images that correlate to the human body. For example, in Nubia there are column in Karnak that resemble the pons and brain stem.

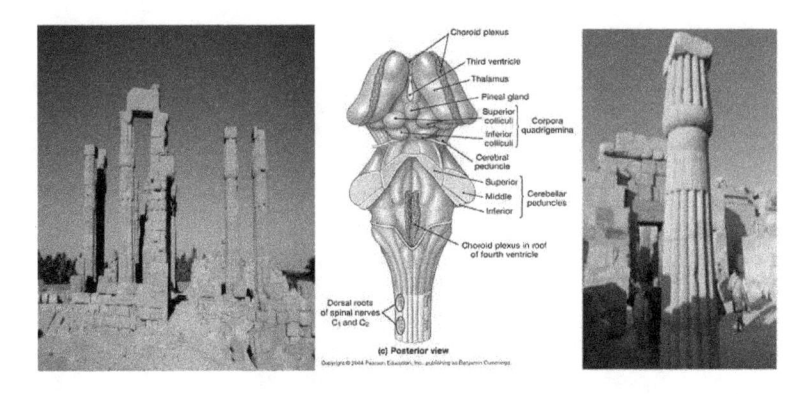

Egyptian Column/Pons

Therefore, it makes sense that ancient names for Egypt like Ta-Kensit which means placenta land, and Alke-bulan mean land of the spirit are use when describing this most ancient country. As this ancient land birthed all cosmologies and Abrahamic religions like Christianity, Judaism and Islam. These three later created their religions based on the same principles of mysticism mixed with physiology and astrology.

There are multiple parts of the brain that are named after Egyptian deities. The hippocampus is also called Ammon's horn. Amun is the ancient deity who part of the Temple of Luxor in Karnak is named after. He along with his consort Mut and son Montu make up the trinity in Karnak whose ancient name was Ipet-isut, meaning "The Most Select (or Sacred) of Places." There is another part of the brain called Putamen (ptah-amun) which is connected to the substantia nigra or black substance. (The science of Melanin, 2nd edition, Moore, Tim, page 37 Zamani Press, Redan, GA 2004).

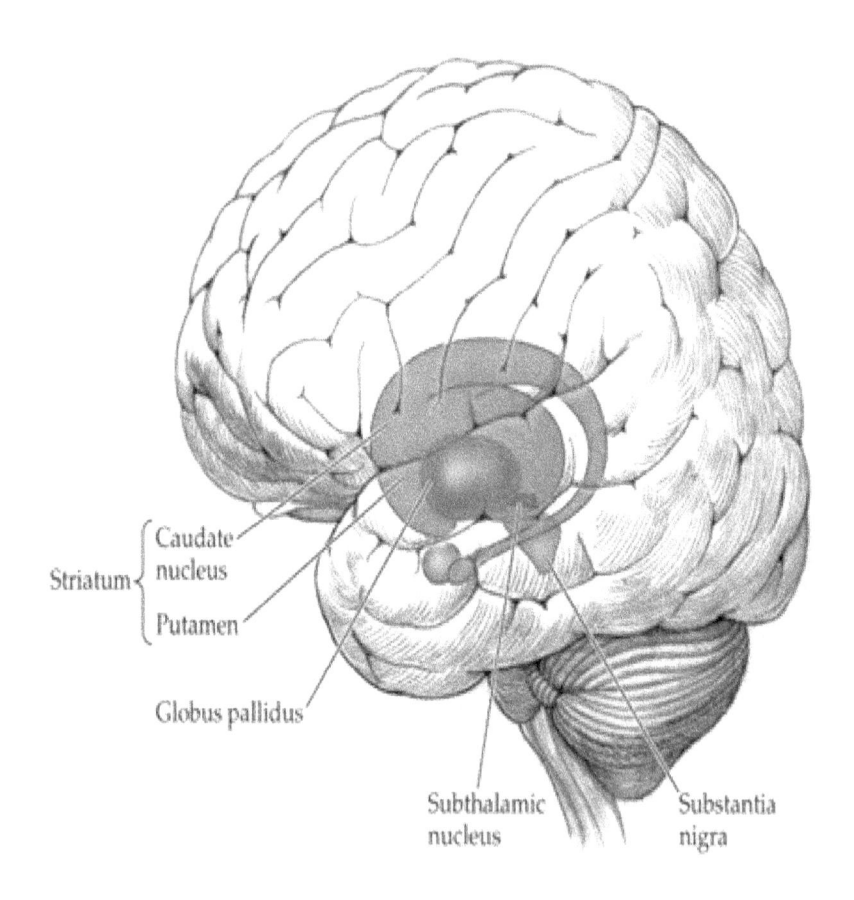

Striatum { Caudate nucleus
Putamen
Globus pallidus
Subthalamic nucleus
Substantia nigra

The Egyptians created images of these parts of the brain and disguised them as deities. For example, what European Americans have called Ammon's horn is

ALLAH, THE QURAN, VENUS AND YOU

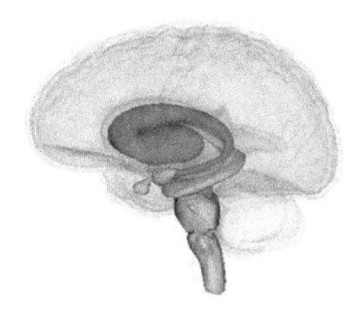

Amun Ra/Hippocampus/Ammon's Horn

actually, symbolized in Egypt as the ram headed deity Amun. Notice how the brainstem is symbolized by the deity under the ram headed sphinx. It is no coincidence this was done by this way as this was symbolic of the reptilian brain which is the oldest of the three brains. The other two are the mammalian and neo-cortex. Thus, Ptah is one of the oldest of the Egyptian deities.

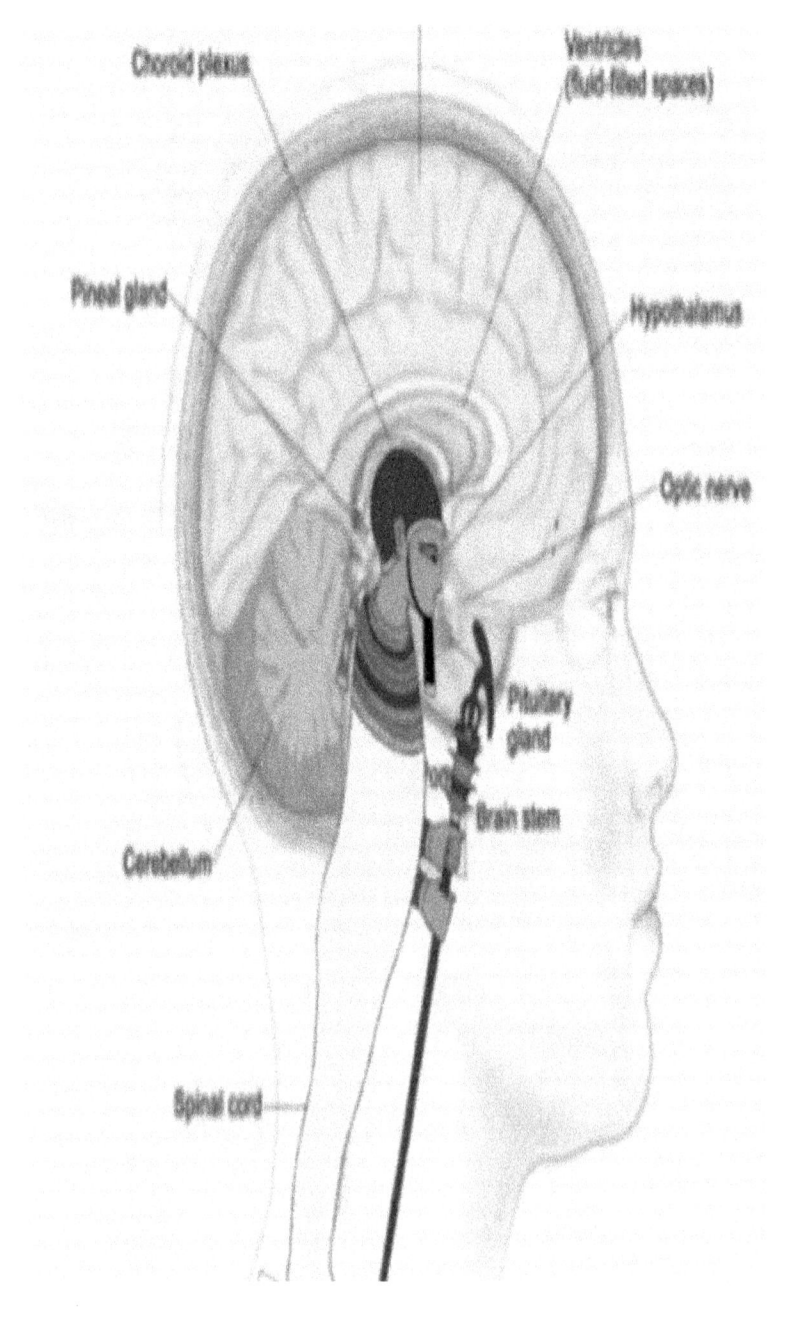

Ptah/Brain Stem

As stated earlier, European used this concept when created their cosmologies and religions to mirror what was illustrated in Egypt. Therefore, it comes as no surprise that attached to Ammon's horn is the amygdala, named after Mary Magdalene. The amygdala is attached to both ends of the hippocampus and is responsible for the fight or flight and euphoria feelings. The word hippocampus means sea horse in the Greek language. This is because it relates to the Greek cosmology of Pegasus the white horse born out of the sea created by the god Poseidon. When you view the hippocampus, it looks like a sea horse. Thus, you can tell how the Greeks copied this concept of using parts of the brain to symbolize their deities in their cosmologies.

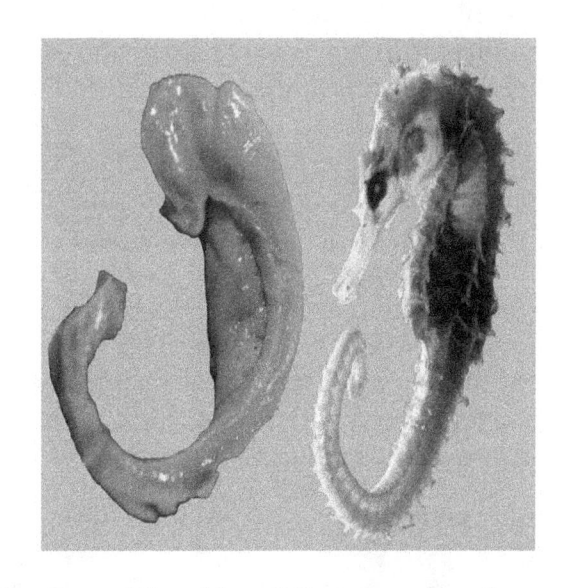

The image of a white horse with wings that could fly also made its way into other cosmologies. Shango is shown with a white horse, Jesus rides a white horse, and the prophet Muhammad rode a steed called the Buraq which had the face of woman, the wings of an eagle. According to the hadith of Bukhari it was described as "Then a white animal which was smaller than a mule and bigger than a donkey was brought to me ... The animal's step (was so wide that it) reached the farthest point within the reach of

ALLAH, THE QURAN, VENUS AND YOU

the animal's sight. Sahih al Bukhari 5:58:227. A hadith is a story allegedly written by the companions of Muhammad. A portion of this story of Muhammad being transported from Mecca to Jerusalem is found in the Quran in Surah Al Isra 17:1 Interestingly, the description of Al Buraq is very similar to the four beasts that surround the throne in the Holy Bible in Revelations 19. These four beasts that surround the throne (sella turcica) represent the four zodiac signs associated with the fixed signs of the zodiac. Scorpio (Eagle-wings), Aquarius (face of a woman), Taurus (bull) and Leo (lion). This is also similar to the Har Em Akhet (Sphinx) which faces the rising sun in the East.

This imagery has been used all over not just in Africa and Greek cosmologies as the Western world use the white horse that is mounted by a hero from where the word Heru comes from. The Lone Ranger rode a female white horse called Silver. The knight always rides the mare. This is also where the word *nightmare* is derived.

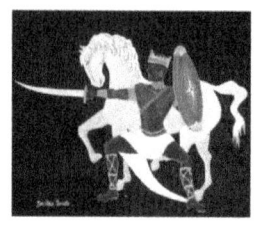

Widow's son and Knight Mare

Physiologically the hippocampus surrounds the pineal gland. The pineal gland represents the hero and masculine aspect, whereas the pituitary represents the wife or feminine aspect along with the amygdala. The amygdala when working with the hippocampus creates sexual feelings and the feeling of religious experiences. The amygdala allows us to feel emotions like love and the euphoria we feel when climaxing. This is the reason Mary Magdalene rubbed Jesus' feet with spikenard an aphrodisiac essential oil. Other essential oils like rose, amber, frankincense and myrrh help to stimulate and sooth the amygdala. When you inhale these scents, it travels through the olfactory, and into the limbic system. As part of the limbic system the amygdala is the only area of the brain that is directly stimulated by external stimulus through the sense of smell by way of the olfactory. Being the source of "divine inspiration" the amygdala was symbolized as the House of God or Bethel in the bible originally it was called Luz a word meaning almond just as the word amygdala means almond or almond shaped.

According to author Picknett in her work "Mary Magdalene" The ancient art of anointing with spikenard oil was part of the ancient pagan ritual of the *hieros gamos* or sacred marriage. The anointing of the head, feet, and genitals "was part of the ritual preparation for penetration during the rite ... in which the priest–king was flooded with the power of the god, while the priestess–queen became possessed by the great goddess (Picknett, *Mary Magdalene*, p. 58). This sacred marriage was symbolic of the marriage between the pituitary and pineal glands. The third part of this is the thalamus a Greek word meaning chamber.

This is the holy trinity of Amun, Mut and Khonsu, Osiris, Isis and Horus, God, Mary and Jesus or lastly Allah, Ar Rahman, and Ar Rahiym. The ancients Africans understood sexuality is a powerful spirit force and allows for access to higher consciousness and spiritual power. This is one of the reason Venus was called the "light-bringer." Using sex magick one can attract their hearts desires and enter enlighten states of consciousness. Thus, when you read the story of Adam, Eve and the snake you begin to understand how the light bringer called Lux Ferre in Latin for Lucifer has been associated with the sex force.

Another anthropomorphic character in Western cosmologies is that of Santa Claus. Santa Claus is a western Christian creation of a character 4th century Greek bishop. According to western legend, Santa Clause comes from the North pole via a sleigh filled with gifts and pulled by eight reindeer. He delivers the gifts to all of those children who have been good all year. So how is this about cosmology you might ask? This story is a play on the cerebral spinal fluid (CSF) called in Greek Chrism. Chrism is also called myrrh and Myron. It is an anointing oil within the Christian tradition. The CSF bathes the brain via the four ventricles and then descends down the spinal column and returns back to the brain. You will find the CSF between the arachnoid mater and the pia mater in the brain. The word arachnoid is derived from the word Arachne meaning spider and oid meaning on the image of. The word mater means mother. Coincidently, in the Quran is surah An Ankabut or the spider Surah 29. In ayyat 41 it states the example of those who take allies other than Allah is like that of the spider who takes a home. And indeed, the weakest of homes is the home of the spider, if they only knew. The arachnoid mater is between the dura matter and pia mater which is thicker and deeper than the arachnoid matter. Surah 29:41 is a direct reference to the weaker and thinner arachnoid matter.

The CSF flows through the pituitary gland and becomes milky white substance. In the pineal gland it is a yellow (gold) substance, or the land of milk and honey. It became the Holy Claus or the Saint Claus bringing gifts from the North pole, aka the head. The head contains the cerebrum. The cerebrum is defined as **cerebrum (n.)** "the brain," 1610s, from Latin cerebrum "the brain" (also "the understanding"), from PIE *keres-, from root *ker- (1) "horn; head." Ker means horn or head and when we define it, it says ker – (1) Proto-Indo-European root meaning "horn; head," with derivatives referring to horned animals, horn-shaped objects, and projecting parts. It forms all or part of: alpenhorn; Capricorn; carat; carotid; carrot; carotene; cerato-; cerebellum; cerebral; cerebrum; cervical; cervix; charivari; cheer; chelicerae; corn (n.2) "hardening of the skin;" cornea; corner; cornet; cornucopia; cranium; flugelhorn; hart; hartebeest; horn; hornbeam; hornblende; hornet; keratin; kerato-; migraine; monoceros; reindeer; rhinoceros; saveloy; serval; triceratops; unicorn.

Notice the definition of reindeer for Ker. The Legend of Santa clause and the reindeer is about the brain. These reindeer are in traditional lore, Santa Claus's sleigh is led by eight reindeer: Dasher, Dancer, Prancer, Vixen, Comet, Cupid, Dunder and Blixem. The names Dunder and Blixem are taken from the words for thunder and lightning. Coincidently, the name Pegasus also means lightning and this is related to the Roman God, Jupiter the God of Thunder. Jupiter is a Latin word meaning Sky God or Jove Pater. Pater is father meaning the Supreme being and is phonetically related to the Egyptian word Ptah.

Also note that Santa Claus is dressed in red, white and black the same color scheme as the sushumna, ida, and pingala. This is hardly a coincidence. As the CSF or Chrism descends down the spinal column and leaves a gift of life in the sacrum so too does Santa descends down the chimney and leaves a gift before ascending up the chimney and back to the north pole. Myrrh, Chrism, CSF or in called in the Hebrew language, shemen is the holy anointing oil that descends down the spinal column into the sacrum and if expelled out the phallus becomes semen, however if retained. It travels up the spinal column back to anoint the pineal gland as shemen.

The pineal gland is also called the epiphysis cerebri. Epiphysis comes to us from the New Latin, from Greek, growth, from *epiphyesthai* to grow on, from *epi-* + *phyesthai* to grow, middle voice of *phyein* to bring forth. This has the same meaning as the word ephiphany.

epiphany (n.)

early 14c., "festival of the manifestation of Christ to the gentiles" (celebrated Jan. 6; usually with a capital -E-), from Old French epiphanie, from Late Latin epiphania, *neuter plural (taken as feminine singular), from late Greek epiphaneia "manifestation, striking appearance, festival held in commemoration of the appearance of a god at some particular place" (in New Testament, "advent or manifestation of Christ"), from epiphanes "manifest, conspicuous," from epiphainein "to manifest, display, show off; come suddenly into view," from epi "on, to" (see epi-) + phainein "to show" (from PIE root *bha- (1) "to shine")*

The reader should begin to see how the names of these body parts are encoded into the cosmologies and religions. Yet it doesn't stop there with pineal gland. Another word used in cosmologies but hidden is the word thalamus. The thalamus along with the pineal and pituitary glands make up the holy trinity. The thalamus would be equated to the child that is produced from the union of the pineal (male) and pituitary (female). Therefore, when we look at the meaning of the word thalamus, we find the following.

thalamus (n.) *plural thalami, 1753, "the receptacle of a flower," Modern Latin, from Latin thalamus "inner chamber, sleeping room" (hence, figuratively, "marriage, wedlock"), from Greek thalamos "inner chamber, bedroom," related to thalame "den, lair," tholos "vault, vaulted building."*

This word has been used in English since 1756 of a part of the forebrain where a nerve appears to originate.

So here we have another gland in the body that relates to the cosmologies of western religions. The inner chamber is from the holies of holies of ark of the covenant. Spoken of in 1 Chronicles 28:11 and also in the book of Exodus the 25th chapter. Exodus 25; [22] "And there I will meet with thee, and I will commune with thee from above the mercy seat, from between the two cherubim's which are upon the ark of the testimony, of all things which I will give thee in commandment unto the children of Israel."

Lalibela

This is the sphenoid bone with the sella turcica that protects the pituitary gland which then connects to the hypothalamus via the infundibulum or pituitary stalk. The religious world believes there was actually an ark that God communicated with Moses and the children of Israel through. The Ethiopians believe they have the ark of the covenant in a church in Axum, Ethiopia. According to Islamic history, Ethiopia is the first place the Prophet Muhammad migrated to escape persecution from Arabs during the early stages of Islam. In Ethiopia is a series of 11 churches that are carved from solid granite. The churches are connected by subterranean passageways. In a placed labelled Lalibela. The interiors were hollowed out into naves and given vaulted ceiling. One of these churches is named Beta Golgotha Michael or the house of the skull

Michael and it contains the remains of its founder Lalibela. Notice the seven steps that lead to the door way of this church.

Symbolically it represents the first seven vertebrae of the spinal column called the cervical vertebrae or superior vertebrae. Golgotha is a Hebrew word meaning skull. In the book of John, it says John19: **[17]** And he bearing his cross went forth into a place called the place of a skull, which is called in the Hebrew Golgotha: These seven superior vertebrae are also related to the seven arch angels. One section at the base of the skull is called Foramen or For Amun, the hidden one. The first of the vertebrae is called Atlas which is the name of the Greek god that carries the world on his shoulders. Atlas was copied after Osiris who was called God of the stairwell. Among the many titles ascribed to Osiris, one frequently used is "the god of the staircase." In Chapter XXII of the Ritual the deceased prays that he may "have a portion with him who is on the top of the staircase," and there are any number of illustrations of a stairway of seven steps. The seven steps are the seven cervical vertebrae. The serpent is the kundalini, and of course Osiris sits on a throne (sella turcica). Notice the Atef crown which represents the olfactory bulb and olfactory tract.

Osiris - God of seven stairs

The oil leaves the brain and then descends down the cervical vertebrae and into spinal column to end up in the sacrum. The Os Sacrum is the Late Latin name meaning sacred bone. It is made up of five bones and these bones eventually fuse together to make the one bone. Once the oil hits this area, it is waiting to be either expelled via the phallus or returned to the brain cavity where it must be crucified around the vagus nerve or the pneumo-gastric nerve which is the 10th of the 12 cranial nerves. Notice the similarity between the esophageal image and that of the ancient Egyptian symbol known as the Sema symbol is the lungs attached to the windpipe. Representing the unification of Upper and Lower Egypt. The same way Narmer was thought to unify Upper and Lower Egypt it was all symbolic of Narmer from the south who fights Serqet (Scorpion king) lower nature and wins which unites lower and upper Egypt aka the lower and higher self. This is the same as what Muslims call jihad. It is simple the internal struggle one has with their thoughts of doing agreeable versus disagreeable.

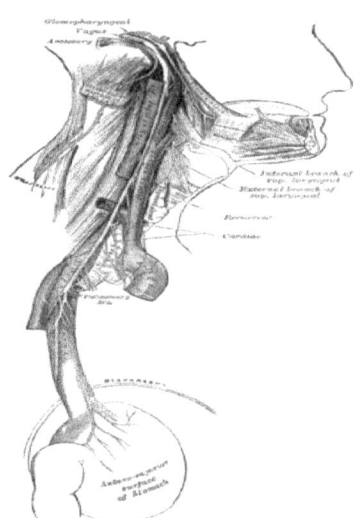

Vagus nerve/Sema

Also note at the top of the Sema is the Neter Khepera the scarab headed deity. His name comes from the Egyptian word, kheprer or "to become". He is the manifestation of the rising sun. The scarab beetle used to identify him is identical to the skull with sutures. This shows you the Egyptians were the initiators of this science of identifying the various portions of the body and associating them with the Neteru (Gods).

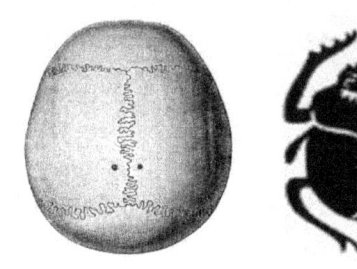

Skull/Khepera

The Sema image shows the two warring deities Heru and Sutukh aka Set. Heru representing the east and the higher nature and Sutukh representing the west or lower nature. Another name for Heru is the KRST or anointed one. The ancient city in Egypt named Cairo from Arabic al-Kahira "the strong," Its older name was khere-ohe, meant "place of combat" which is in reference to battle between the Heru and Sutukh. Its official name *al-Qāhirah* (Arabic: القاهرة) means "the Vanquisher" or "the Conqueror", supposedly due to the fact that the planet Mars, al-Najm al-Qahir (Arabic: النجم القاهر, literally "the Counquering Star"), was rising at the time when the city was founded
https://www.etymonline.com/word/Cairo#etymonline_v_25806

In the science of iatromatematics or medical astrology the 12 zodiac signs rule the body. The head is ruled by Aries, the throat by Taurus, arms by Gemini, chest by Cancer, Leo rules the heart, Virgo the stomach, Libra the kidneys, Scorpio rules the genital region where the os sacrum is located, Sagittarius rules the hips, the knees are ruled by Capricorn, shins by Aquarius and lastly the feet by Pisces. Thus, using this model, Serqet the scorpion deity is ruled by Scorpio or the lower nature in the genital region and Narmer the head the higher nature. Therefore, Heru would be equal to Aries and Sutukh whose color is red represents the lower nature or near where Scorpio rules in the body.

The ancient Egyptians used various zoo types to symbolize particular concepts, such as the Vulture (motherhood); the Beetle (transformation, evolution and rebirth) and the Falcon or Hawk (wisdom). The vulture is used because it takes amazing care of its young and represents the mother aspect as well as protection. Author Athanasius Kircher wrote 'Oedipus Aegyptiacus' says, "The spinal cord was symbolized by a snake, and the serpent coiled upon the foreheads of the Egyptian initiates represented the Divine Fire which had crawled serpent-like up the Tree of Life". (Kirshner, Athanasius, Oedipus Aegyptiacus, 2002, p.31.) The Kabbalist took the Ka, Ba, and the Akh all symbols of the soul to create the Kabballah (Ka-Ba-Akh) and its traditions. The vulture represents the air and the serpent represents the land again showing duality. Duality is as well physiological for the brain and the stomach are made of the same tissue.

Lately, physicians have noted that constipation is one of the most common symptoms of Parkinson's disease patients. Constipation affects roughly one half of the individuals diagnosed with the Parkinson's or other neurodegenerative condition. Where initially physicians treated Parkinson's as a disease that affects the brain, more are now beginning to study the gastrointestinal tract as a source of neurodegenerative diseases. In 2003, German neuroanatomist Heiko Braak who worked at the University of Ulm in Germany, and his colleagues proposed that Parkinson's may actually originate in the gut rather than the brain. Researchers believe the pathological agents or bad gut bacteria travel from the stomach to the brain via the vagus nerve or Sema symbol.

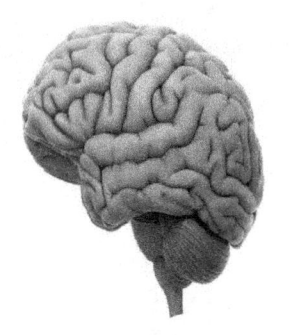

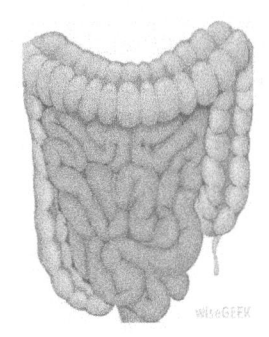

Brain/Stomach

It is imperative that you maintain good stomach or gut bacteria to ensure this debilitative disease does not affect you. Since studies have shown roughly half of all those studied with Parkinson's suffered from constipation, to lessen the chances of getting Parkinson's one should eliminate waste at least daily. As mentioned in the scroll, *God, the Bible, the Planets and your Body*, the stomach is called the belly from the Latin word abdomen and the gut. These again are names for the various deities. Belly is Ba'al, abdomen (slave of the omen) and Gut comes from the German word Gott which became God. This takes us back to the story of the God of the bible giving the children of Israel manna as they wondered in the desert for 40 years.

The Book of Exodus 16:31 And the house of Israel called the name thereof Manna; and it was like coriander seed, white; and the taste of it was like wafers made with honey.

לֹא, וַיִּקְרְאוּ בֵית-יִשְׂרָאֵל אֶת-שְׁמוֹ, מָן; וְהוּא, כְּזֶרַע גַּד לָבָן וְטַעְמוֹ, כְּצַפִּיחִת בִּדְבָשׁ

Exodus states that raw manna tasted like wafers that had been made with honey. The word *mana* appears three times in the Quran, in Quran 2:57, And We shaded you with clouds and sent down to you manna and quails, [saying], "Eat from the good things with which We have provided you." And they wronged Us not - but they were [only] wronging themselves. Manna is also found in Surah 7:160 and 20:80. The word manna is of the root of mannite which means sugar. This sugar that comes from Heaven or the head is called Galactose or brain sugar. Galactose is a milky sugary substance. The Holy Bible tells us the Israelites ground manna and pounded it into cakes, which were then baked, resulting in something that tasted like cakes baked with oil. This is simply esoterism as we live in the Milky Way galaxy or the land of milk and honey. Via which the pineal gland gives us the golden substance and the pituitary gland gives us the milky white substance.

We are told we only use 10% of our brains and the remaining 90% goes pretty much unused. Correspondingly the visible universe constitutes roughly 10% of what we see. The other 90% is mainly dark matter and dark energy. The Holy Bible tells us God dwells in darkness Amos 5:18 Woe unto you that desire the day of the LORD! to what end is it for you? the day of the LORD is darkness, and not light. Amos 5:20 Shall not the day of the LORD be darkness, and not light? even very dark, and no brightness in it?

כ. הֲלֹא-חֹשֶׁךְ יוֹם יְהוָה, וְלֹא-אוֹר; וְאָפֵל, וְלֹא-נֹגַהּ לוֹ

Psalms 18:11 "He made darkness his secret place; his pavilion round about him were dark waters and thick clouds of the skies."

יב יָשֶׁת חֹשֶׁךְ, סִתְרוֹ-- סְבִיבוֹתָיו סֻכָּתוֹ
חֶשְׁכַת-מַיִם, עָבֵי שְׁחָקִים.

    Since God dwells in darkness it stands to reason why his High Priest is called Melchizedek the King of Peace. The dark energy/matter is peaceful and still. Therefore, when one goes into meditation it should be quiet and still. This allow the chrism to flow black into the land of milk and honey from the wilderness (gut). Abraham brought a tenth of all to Melchizedek. Mel is short for melanin or dark/black. Chi is energy and is represented in Greek as X; Z represents the number of protons in the nucleus of an atom; it indicates the position of the element in the periodic system. Dek/Dec meaning tenth. This is why Abraham brought a tenth of all to Melchizedek. It is referring to what happens when you meditate in darkness, the pineal gland secretes serotonin. Approximately 90% of serotonin is located in the gastrointestinal track which regulates intestinal movements. Serotonin is primarily found in the enteric nervous system which is called the second brain as it can function independently of the central nervous system.

RED BLACK AND WHITE

The Originator Surah 35.27. Do you not see that Allah sends down water from the cloud, then We bring forth therewith fruits of various colors; and in the mountains are streaks, white and red, of various hues and (others) intensely black?

The ida is white for the moon, pingala is red for the sun, sushumna is black for the heavens and last is the color green or gold for Venus. Venus is associated with the metal Copper which has a gold or tan hue. The moon pulls on the water in our bodies and affects our emotional self, whereas the sun pulls on our psyche and mental self. This color scheme is adopted by the first group of Christians and eventually the Roman Catholic Church. Members of the Catholic church should recognize this as the Pope who represents Allah the feminine principle wears white. The Cardinals wear red and represent the male aspect like a beehive which only has one queen and man male drone bees. Lastly the priests wear black representative of the sushumna or spinal column which supports the body.

Another example is the description of the four horses of the apocalypse. Before we get into those, we should first understand the word apocalypses has been grossly misinterpreted by the religious world to mean the end of the world by way of some divine destruction. This is incorrect the word literally means to uncover, to reveal as John the Revelator was doing talking about the end of the Piscean age not the entire world. Now these four horses are representative of the four cardinal points and zodiac elements.

In the book of Revelations 6:[1] And I saw when the Lamb opened one of the seals, and I heard, as it were the noise of thunder, one of the four beasts saying, Come and see. [2] And I saw, and behold a white horse: and he that sat on him had a bow; and a crown was given unto him: and he went forth conquering, and to conquer. [3] And when he had opened the second seal, I heard the second beast say, Come and see. [4] And there went out another horse that was red: and power was given to him that sat thereon to take peace from the earth, and that they should kill one another: and there was given unto him a great sword. [5] And when he had opened the third seal, I heard the third beast say, Come and see. And I beheld, and lo a black horse; and he that sat on him had a pair of balances in his hand. [6] And I heard a voice in the midst of the four beasts say, A measure of wheat for a penny, and three measures of barley for a penny; and see thou hurt not the oil and the wine. [7] And when he had opened the fourth seal, I heard the voice of the fourth beast say, Come and see. [8] And I looked, and behold a pale horse: and his name that sat on him was Death, and Hell followed with him. And power was given unto them over the fourth part of the earth, to kill with sword, and with hunger, and with death, and with the beasts of the earth. The seals being discussed here are the chakras.

The first horse is white and has a bow representative of Aries the god of war. The second horse was red which represents Cancer for it is the emotional body which has the power to take peace from the Earth. The third horse was black and the rider had a pair of scales. This is the symbol of Ma'at in Egypt but called by westerners Libra whose symbol is also a pair of scales. The last and final horse is pale representative of the winter time and death because all vegetation and sometimes human life dies during the winter. The Black horse is Libra, and the Pale horse is Capricorn, Aries is the white horse, and Cancer is the red horse.

Four horses of the Apocalypse

These colors are having been used in ancient Egypt and Africa for millennia also represent the Hebrew God YHWH; Yod is fire, Heh is water, Wow is air and Heh is earth. This is the original fantastic four also known as

Tamunefuset; Ta – earth, mu – water, nefu – water and set – fire. Symbolized in the Sudan via the black, red, green flag of the Ansaars led by the Mahdi, Muhammad Ahmed who practiced an esoteric version of Islam and followed a Sufi order called the Samaniyya order. This flag was used by Duse Ali, who influenced the Most Honorable Marcus Garvey as well as Nobel Drew Ali. Now the color scheme has been switched by those calling themselves RBG (Red Black Green), yet the original color was Black, Red, Green with a white spear and crescent.

Flag of the Mahdi

The green, white, and gold are interchangeable as they represent Venus the goddess of love. Egyptians have a similar flag. In the Yoruba tradition and the spiritual tradition of Ifa these colors are used

- the green for correspond to East, Light, Fire
- the blue for correspond to West, Dark, Water
- the black for correspond to North, Heaven
- the red for correspond to South, Earth

The Orisha are usually shown together in white. However, they have also been represented by the colors red or black in other instances. Individually they are associated with various colors. For instance, the Orisha called Oshun/Osun has been associated with the color yellow.

ALLAH, THE QURAN, VENUS AND YOU

Oshun is commonly called the river Orisha, or goddess, and is typically associated with water, purity, fertility, love, and sensuality. Another Orisha is Yemaya and she is the goddess of the sea and salt water, whereas her sister Osun is the goddess of the river and fresh water. Offerings to Oshun include sweet things such as honey, mead, white wine, oranges, sweets or pumpkins. This association with honey brings an interesting connection, for the male Honey bee has 16 chromosomes. Surah 16 of the Quran is An Nahl meaning The Bee. It has a total of 128 verses which is a multiple of 256 or 16 x 16. The paths of Ifa are 16 and each path has 16 more paths for a total of 256 steps/paths. Starting with you, there are 9 generations until you get to your 256 ancestors. (2, 4, 8, 16, 32, 64, 128, 256).

Going back in time you start to notice again the correspondence between the stars, Gods and humans in Egyptian cosmology as everything was based on the stars and the way the Egyptians tracked these stars. For instance, it is relayed that Heru (Horus) took 12 steps, this represents the 12 hours of the day. The word Hours came from the word Horus, as did Minutes came from the deity Min and lastly Set is associated with sunset. The Gods/star were essentially used to tell time. Sirius was recorded and tracked to let them know when the Hapi (Nile) river would flood annually. Using the correspondence of As above so Below, we must now look at our bodies to see if we also are associated with time. There are 13 lunar cycles in a lunar year which relate to the 13 menstrual cycles child bearing women have monthly. The lunar month can be divided into two 14 days cycles, one waxing and one waning period. Thus, one way to calculate the month is by using the phalanges on the hand. Each hand has 14 phalanges for a total of 28 phalanges equaling the amount of days in the average lunar rotation. 14 on the left hand the waning moon and 14 on the right hand for the waxing moon. This also correlates to the 28 Arabic alphabet with 14 moon letters and 14 sun letters. The English alphabet has 26 alphabet and your foot has 26 bones. The Hebrew alphabet has 22 characters and your head has 22 bones. These three equals 72 which equates to the amount of years it takes the sun to move 1 degree on its 360-degree rotation through the kosmos.

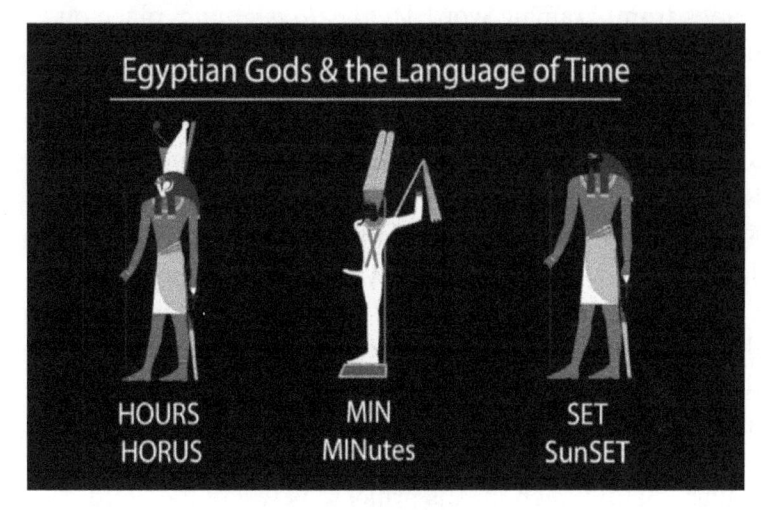

Gods of Time

The Holy Bible states in Genesis 1:14 "And God said, Let there be lights in the firmament of the heaven to divide the day from the night; and let them be for signs, and for seasons, and for days, and years:"

וַיֹּאמֶר אֱלֹהִים, יְהִי מְאֹרֹת בִּרְקִיעַ הַשָּׁמַיִם, לְהַבְדִּיל, בֵּין הַיּוֹם וּבֵין הַלָּיְלָה; וְהָיוּ לְאֹתֹת וּלְמוֹעֲדִים, וּלְיָמִים וְשָׁנִים

The Hebrew calendar starts counting from Adam and the Gregorian calendar starts counting from Jesus. The Islamic calendar starts from the date Muhammad made his migration from Mecca to Medina and is known as hijra. Another calendar that exist is the freemason calendar that is has 39-year difference from the Hebrew calendar.

In conclusion Venus has an extensive association with Islam and the great feminine energy. The divine mother has historically been the oldest of deities and prior to the appearance of patriarchal religions was the only deity. This religion is called Din from Dinah or the Din Allah. From Allah to Dinah, Sophia on to Mary Magdalene, the wife of Jesus, Mary Magdalene, which comes from Aramaic word *Maghdela meaning*, place on the Sea of Galilee. Galilee means circle and Jesus was from Galilee meaning the circle. Or seen astrologically, the sun comes from the sea of the circle another way to say the zodiac on the ecliptic. Physiologically this is represented by the Amygdala a gland at both ends of the hippocampus. Mary's sister was Martha and they had a disagreement over Jesus Luke 10:40 But Martha was cumbered about much serving, and came to him, and said, Lord, dost thou not care that my sister hath left me to serve alone? bid her therefore that she help me. This two-sister theme begins with Aset and Nebthys, extends to Eve and Lilith, the wives of Adam and goes even further to wives of Abraham, Sarai and Hagar. Sarai which means princess is where the word Syria derives and the word Assyria means Land of Venus. Again, physiologically this is found in the brain as the dura mater meaning hard mother and pia mater meaning soft mother. As you study the stories of the polygamous marriages of all these cosmologies, you will notice there is the duality of the two women/wives. The same way the moon has a waxing and waning period. Therefore, there was an abundance of feminine energy to overpower the masculine energy and accounts for why the Quran deals with love (Venus) and peace (Taurus) yet at times war (Mars). Astrologically Venus along with Mercury, is never far away from the Sun, just as thinking (Mercury) and your values (Venus) are never far removed from yourself (the Sun).

ALLAH, THE QURAN, VENUS AND YOU

Venus is associated with the number six which deals with the divine mother, protection and the mother wit. Six is associated with copper and the second to the last day of the week Friday. The holiest day of the week in Islam is Jummah and corresponds to Friday in Western calendars. The Quran has a total of 114 books which equals 6 (1+1+4=6) and 114 divided by 6 is 19. The Quran was revealed over a period of 23 years according to Islamic history (2*3 = 6). It takes Venus 224.7 days to rotate around the sun (2+2+4+7 = 15 1+5 = 6). Venus rotates clockwise which makes the Sun rise in the West as opposed to the East like on Earth. Thus, according to this Hadith this is referencing Venus Sahih Bukhari: Volume 04, Book 54, Number 421

Narrated Abu Dhar:

The Prophet asked me at sunset, "Do you know where the sun goes (at the time of sunset)?" I replied, "Allah and His Apostle know better." He said, "It goes (i.e. travels) till <u>it prostrates</u> itself underneath the Throne and <u>takes the permission to rise again</u>, and it is permitted and then (a time will come when) it will be about to prostrate itself but its prostration will not be accepted, and it will ask permission to go on its course but it will not be permitted, but it will be ordered to return whence it has come and so <u>it will RISE IN THE WEST</u>. And that is the interpretation of the Statement of Allah:

In addition, the alchemical color of Venus is green and the Qurans of the Islamic world are mostly green. Islamic tradition speaks about a mystical character name Al Khidr meaning the green one who is the spiritual guide of

Musa (Moses, Moshe). The tomb of the Arabian prophet Muhammad is also green.

The Din of Islam or Din of Allah has its adherents praying based on the movement of the sun as well as in relationship the 7 chakras. They circumvent a black cube seven times to mimic the seven spinning chakras. Proverbs 9:1 says, "Wisdom hath built herself a house, she hath hewn her out seven pillars. חָכְמוֹת, בָּנְתָה בֵיתָהּ ; חָצְבָה עַמּוּדֶיהָ שִׁבְעָה. Wisdom is the word Hikmah in Hebrew and has the feminine ending "ah" this is why this verse speaks in the feminine. Later Muslims built a house of wisdom dedicated to the feminine deity Allah/Allat sometimes referred to as Saturn (El) whose color is black. Hikmah and Sophia are both feminine words dealing wisdom. Sophia gives us the word philosophy meaning love of wisdom and the prophet Muhammad advises Muslims to seek knowledge from the cradle to the grave.

ALLAH, THE QURAN, VENUS AND YOU

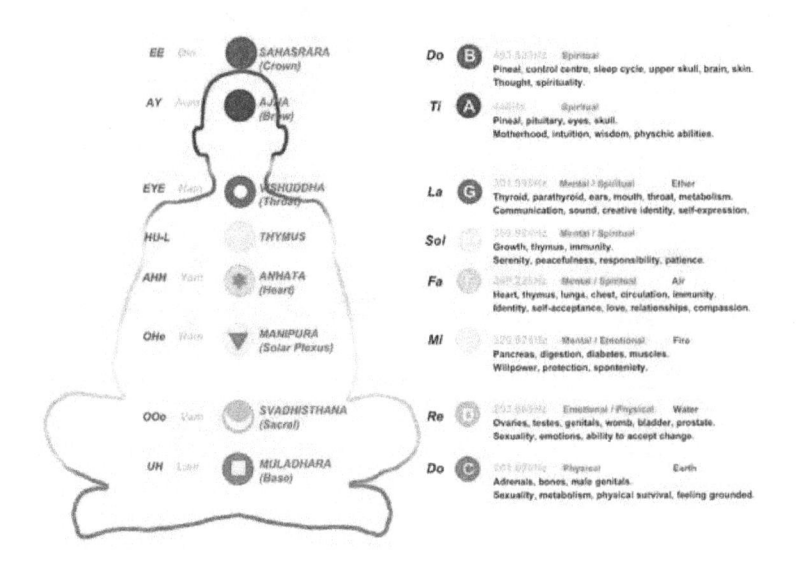

ALLAH, THE QURAN, VENUS AND YOU

Category	Red	Orange	Yellow	Green	Blue	Indigo	Violet
Chakra	Root	Sacral	Solar Plexus	Heart	Throat	Thrid Eye	Crown
Connected To	Physical Self	Emotional Self	Mental Self	Unconditional Love	Holistic Thought	Unconditional Self	Spiritual self
Affirmation	"I Will"	"I Feel"	"I Can"	"I Love"	"I Speak"	"I See"	"I Know"
Personality Traits	Strong Willed Inplusive	Extroverted, Happy	Intellectua, Practical	Nature, Loving, Romantic	Caring, Curious	Wise, Truth Seeker	itive,Creative,Insperat
Qualities	Vitality, Courage, Confidence, Strength, Security, Will-Power	Joy,Resourcefulnes s,Removed Inhibitons & Limitation	Wisdom,Clarity,Self Esteem,Curiosity,A wareness	Balance, Self-control,Harmony,Rene wal,Understanding	Knowledge,Health,De cisivness,Truth,Loyalt y,Communication	Intuition,Understa nding,Fearless,He aliaf,Fulfilment	Self-Sacrificing,Creativity, Visionary,Strong Mentally
Gland	Adrenal	Reproductive Organs	Pancreas	Thymus	Thyroid	Pituitary	Pineal
Physically Gives Energy To Help	Legs,Feet,Vagina& Urinary Organs, Tiredness, Anemia,Blood Disorders	Respiroty,Spleen,K idney&Gall Bladder, Recharges Etheric Body/Aura	Digestion,Liver,Dia betes&Skin, Poor Digestion&Nervous ness	Heart,Bronchia,Lungs, Arms & Legs, Chronic Disease and Hypertension	Neck & Voice, Reduces Fevers, Hyperactivity, Insomnia & Menstrul Problems	Pineal Gland & Nervous System, Increases Psychic Abilities, Heals Body/Aura	Lymphatic System, Kills Bacteria & Heals Skin Rashes, Emotional Issues
Complementary	Blue	Indigo	Violet	Red/Magenta	Red	Orange	Yellow
Day Of The Week	Tuesday	Wednesday	Sunday	Friday	Thrusday	Saturday	Monday
Element	Earth	Water	Fire	Air	Ether	Light	Spirit
Sense	Smell	Taste	Sight	Touch	Hearing	intuition	Knowingness
Musical Note/Sound	C Note/Oo	D Note/Oh	E Note/Aw	F Note/Ah	G Note/Eh	A Note/Ih	B Note/Eee
Gemstone	Red Tiger's Eye	Carnelian	Citrine	Aventurine	Sodalite	Amethyst	Quartz Crystal
Essential Oils	Ylang Ylang	Melissa/Orange	Rosemary	Encaplytus/Pine	Gernaium	Patchouli	Lavender

Pronunciation

Ee – Egypt - me

Aa – Amen - say

Eye – Isis - my

Ah – Ausar - saw

Oh – - go

Oo - Hu - you

Uh - (Tut) cup

Ruling Planet Frequency

♄ Saturn 768

♃ Jupiter 720

♂ Mars 672

☉ Sun 624

♀ Venus 528

☿ Mercury 480

☾ Moon 432

PICUTRES/IMAGES

The Prophet Muhammad

Fatima, daughter of Muhammad

Five Pillars

Duse Ali

Moorish Science Temple of America (MSTA)

Master Fard Muhammad

President Barack Hussein Obama

Malcolm X

The Honorable Elijah Muhummad

Dr. Martin Luther King, Jr

Sheik Daoud Ahmad Faisal

As Sayid Al Imaam Isa Al Haadi, Al Mahdi

Kalima/Shahadah

Prostration Mark

Hatim

Siva Lingam

Tefillin

Platonic Solids

Aphrodite

Pope learning Astrology

Sun/Moon Letters

Phalanges

Seat of Light/Chakras

Pharoah Tutankhamun (King Tut)

Nadis

Yoga/Salaat

Egyptian Women playing Harp

Music Chart

Het Heru (Hathor)

Planets/Pyramids

Allah and first woman

Al Fatihah

Ka'aba Black Stone

ALLAH, THE QURAN, VENUS AND YOU

- Kissing the feet of St. Peter/Kissing Black Stone
- Vesica Pisis
- Pillars in the Ka'aba
- Tomb of Muhammad
- Sirius A/B rotation
- Muhammad Seal of the Prophets
- Zodiac Calendar
- Five levels of consciousness
- Olfactory System
- Three Wise Men
- Essentials Oils Chart
- Nabta Playa

- Skull and Bones
- Sah/Orion
- Virgo/Aset
- Temple of Aset
- Aset
- Sphenoid Bone
- Ankh/Anchor
- Ventral View of the Brain
- Olfactory Bulb
- Atef Crown
- Egyptian Columns/Pons Brain
- Amun Ra/Hippocampus/Ammon's Horn

- Ptah/Brain Stem
- Seahorse/Hippocampus
- Santa Claus
- Widow's son and Knight Mare
- Lalibela
- Osiris – God of the seven stairs
- Vagus nerve/Sema
- Skull/Khepera
- Brain/Stomach
- Cardinal
- Four horses of the Apocalypse
- Flag of the Mahdi
- Gods of Time

CITED WORKS

Al Mahdi, As Sayyid Al Imaam Isa Haadi, Qur'aanic Arabic Lessons for The Nubian Islaamic Hebrews, Nubian Islaamic Hebrews Ansaaru Allah Publication, Brooklyn, NY, 1986, (pgs 8a-9a)

Axe, Joshua, Essential Oils, Ancient Medicine. Axe Wellness LLC, (2016) p.46

András J. E. Bodrogligeti, *A Grammar of Chagatay* (2001)

The Quick and the Dead: Biomedical Theory in Ancient Egypt First Edition. Brill/Styx. ISBN 90-04-12391-1.

Tony Bushby, The Crucifixion of the Truth, p. 166.

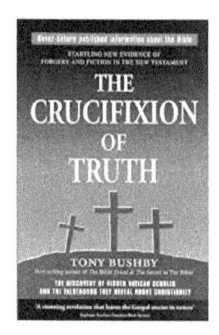

Andrews, Ted, (Dictionary of Symbols, Chevalier & Gheerbrant; Animal Speak, 2002, page 29

Gehl, Jennifer, The Planetary Signatures in Medicine, Restoring the Cosmic Foundation of Healing, Healing Arts Press, (2017), page 87

David Dabydeen, John Gilmore, Cecily Jones (eds), *The Oxford Companion to Black British History*, Oxford University Press, 2007, p. 25.

Manly P. Hall (1901-1990) in his *Secret Teachings of All Ages* discusses the correspondences: Manly P. Hall. *Secret Teachings of All Ages* (New York, NE:Tarcher/Penguin, 2003[1928]).

Ireneaus, Against Heresies, Wm B. Eerdsman Publishing, 1885, pg 21

Kirshner, Athanasius, Oedipus Aegyptiacus, 2002, p.31.)

Islam and the Arabs, Rom Landau, 1958 p 11-21

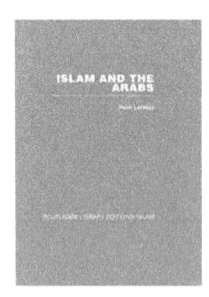

(McLean, The Triple Goddess, 80.) The Triple Goddess: An Exploration of the Archetypal Feminine (Hermetic Research Series) Paperback – June 1, 1989 by Adam McLean.

The science of Melanin, 2nd edition, Moore, Tim, page 37 Zamani Press, Redan, GA 2004).

"Muhammad, Elijah, The University of Islam, Chicago, Illinois, 1957, The Supreme Wisdom, Page 11

Nurbaki, Haluk, Verses from the Holy Quran and the Facts of Science, Kitab Bhavan Publishing, 2007, page 88

Rooakhptah Amunnubi, The Degree of Muhummadism, Tama-Re Publishing, 2001, p. 40.

Schneider, Stephen (2009). Pathways to Astrology: New York, NY McGraw-Hill Companies Publishing. p. 311. ISBN 978-0-07-340445-5

Dr. David Stewart, author of Healing Oils of the Bible

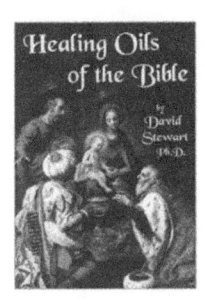

Strong, James, Strong's, Exhaustive Concordance of the Bible. Publisher: Hendrickson Publishers, Incorporated, 2009

Sahih al Bukhari: Volume 04, Book 54, Number 421

Sahih al Bukhari 5:58:227

Stedmans, Stedman's Medical Dictionary, 2001, ISBN-13: 978-1608316922

Wehr, Hans, Arabic-English Dictionary: The Hans Wehr Dictionary of Modern Written Arabic (English and Arabic Edition) 1800

York, Malachi, Shaikh Daoud V. W.D. Ward, Holy Tabernacle Ministries Publishing. 1999, p.118

York, Malachi, The Science of Healing, Holy Tabernacle Ministries Publishing, 1998, p.47

https://aromawealth.com/raise-your-energy-frequency-with-essential-oils/ taken 9/3/2018

https://biblehub.com/hebrew/2142.htm taken 5/3/2018

https://biblehub.com/str/hebrew/8081.htm taken 5/3/2018

http://www.eliyah.com/cgi-bin/strongs.cgi?file=hebrewlexicon&isindex=7699 taken 5/3/2018

http://www.eliyah.com/cgi-bin/strongs.cgi?file=hebrewlexicon&isindex=193 taken 6/29/2018

https://www.etymonline.com/word/isotope#etymonline_v_12274 taken 8/3/2018

https://www.etymonline.com/word/Cairo#etymonline_v_25806 taken 8/3/2018

https://www.etymonline.com/word/Allah#etymonline_v_8165 taken 9/08/2018 https://www.etymonline.com/word/yawn#etymonline_v_44484 taken 10/1/2018

https://www.etymonline.com/word/orchid#etymonline_v_7121 taken 10/1/2018

https://www.etymonline.com/word/vanilla#etymonline_v_4632 taken 10/1/2018

https://www.etymonline.com/word/vagina#etymonline_v_4600 taken 10/1/2018

https://www.etymonline.com/word/seminar#etymonline_v_23190 taken 10/1/2018

https://www.etymonline.com/word/avocado#etymonline_v_19006 taken 10/1/2018

https://www.etymonline.com/word/*gwen-#etymonline_v_52790 taken 10/1/2018

,
https://www.etymonline.com/word/yawn#etymonline_v_44484 taken 10/1/2018

https://www.etymonline.com/word/Argonaut#etymonline_v_26507 taken 10/1/2018

http://www.fuccha.in/namaaz-yoga-of-islamic-prayer-and-its-medical-benefits taken 8/26/2018

http://gnosis.org/library/advh1.htm taken 7/5/2018

http://www.heavenlyscent.net/frequency.htm taken 3/6/17

https://www.merriam-webster.com/dictionary/parable taken 9/19/2018.

http://www.mechon-mamre.org/ taken 3/1/2019

https://www.nasa.gov/feature/goddard/2018/sounds-of-the-sun taken 9/30/2018

http://www.truthbeknown.com/islam.htm   taken 9/15/18

https://quran.com taken 3/1/2019

ALLAH, THE QURAN, VENUS AND YOU

NOTES

ALLAH, THE QURAN, VENUS AND YOU

ALLAH, THE QURAN, VENUS AND YOU

CPSIA information can be obtained
at www.ICGtesting.com
Printed in the USA
BVHW080809070720
582997BV00002B/302